Higher Ground

A Call for Christian Civility

Russell Dilday

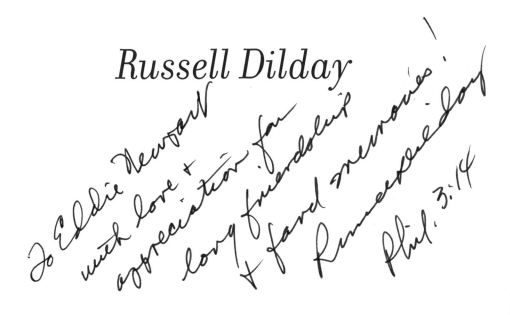

Smyth & Helwys Publishing, Inc.
6316 Peake Road
Macon, Georgia 31210-3960
1-800-747-3016
©2007 by Smyth & Helwys Publishing
All rights reserved.
Printed in the United States of America.

The paper used in this publication meets the minimum requirements of
American National Standard for Information Sciences—
Permanence of Paper for Printed Library Materials.
ANSI Z39.48–1984. (alk. paper)

Library of Congress Cataloging-in-Publication Data

Dilday, Russell H.
Higher Ground : A Call for Christian Civility
by Russell Dilday.
p. cm.
ISBN 978-1-57312-469-0 (pbk. : alk. paper)
1. Courtesy.
2. Conduct of life.
3. Christian life.
I. Title.
BJ1533.C9D55 2007
241'.671—dc22

2006039618

Contents

Dedicated to David and Charis Smith,
gracious and genuine followers of Christ
who embody the Christian civility called for
in *Higher Ground*. Their encouragement
and support helped bring this book
from concept to reality.

Preface

One of the program highlights of the Southern Baptist Convention (SBC) meeting each year is the Convention sermon. It's one of the best-attended sessions, and to be invited to bring the annual sermon is a distinct honor. So it was a pleasant surprise when the committee responsible for recommending the preacher for the 1984 Convention contacted me early in 1983. They asked permission to submit my name at the Convention meeting in Pittsburgh, Pennsylvania, on June 11, 1983, for approval to preach the Convention sermon in 1984. Ironically, at that Pittsburgh meeting, fundamentalist Jimmy Draper was elected to a second term as SBC president, and another fundamentalist, Charles Stanley, pastor of First Baptist Church, Atlanta, Georgia, was elected president of the Pastor's Conference. This latter position had become the stepping-stone for election the ensuing year as president of the SBC. Stanley's election in 1984 as SBC president confirmed that pattern.

Even though the fundamentalists were there to elect these and others of their candidates, and even though I had already begun to speak out publicly against the methodology of the takeover efforts, there was no opposition to the committee's nomination. I began a year-long process of preparing a sermon for Baptists who would gather in Kansas City in June 1984.

It was truly an awesome responsibility. Until then, the only other seminary president elected to preach the annual Convention sermon was E. Y. Mullins, president of Southern Seminary in 1901. Mullins, who ranks high on my "most admired Baptist" list, was the subject of my PhD dissertation at Southwestern, *The Apologetic Method of E. Y. Mullins*.

I struggled with two choices. I could pick a generic theme, choose a noncontroversial text, and preach a "safe" inspirational message, even recycling one of my old sermons, or I could try to address the current tensions in the denomination and challenge Baptists to move beyond the morass and get back to the ultimate purposes of the Convention: evangelism and missions.

Needless to say, I prayed a lot. Several months went by as I explored the first option and then cautiously considered the possibilities of the second. I had no ambitions of being a bold prophet and certainly no inclination to become a denominational martyr, but more and more I was drawn to the certainty that this providential time in Baptist life called for a unique message. The dictionary definition of preaching is "to deliver, to advocate, to urge strongly, persistently." It was obvious to me that this was the time to do just that.

Setting aside a week on the seminary calendar when I could give full attention to preparing the message, I gathered my notes, commentaries, and yellow legal pads (my antiquated Tandy computer was called a portable, but it really wasn't) and headed to a condominium at April Sound on Lake Conroe in south Texas. One of my favorite personal devotional times when I talk to the Lord and worship is the time I spend alone behind the wheel of my car on the interstate. I play Christian music, sing, think, pray, and listen for any insights from God. On the way down I-45 to Conroe in my "rolling prayer closet," the tape player began to play an arrangement of one of my favorite hymns, "Higher Ground," written by Johnson Oatman, Jr., in 1892.

> I'm pressing on the upward way, new heights I'm gaining every day;
> Still praying as I onward bound, "Lord plant my feet on higher
>   ground."
> My heart has no desire to stay, where doubts arise and fears dismay;
> Though some may dwell where these abound, my prayer, my aim is
>   higher ground.
> I want to live above the world, though Satan's darts at me are
>   hurled;
> For faith has caught the joyful sound, the song of saints on higher
>   ground.
> I want to scale the utmost height, and catch a gleam of glory bright;
> But still I'll pray till heaven I've found, "Lord, lead me on to higher
>   ground."
> Lord, lift me up and help me stand, by faith on Heaven's tableland;

A higher plane than I have found, Lord, plant my feet on higher
    ground.

In one of those rare flashes of insight, sparked I believe by the
Holy Spirit, I realized this was my theme. We Baptists needed to move
beyond the lowlands of caustic controversy to the higher ground of
Christian civility. Almost immediately I thought of the biblical texts in
Philippians 3:14, "I press on toward the goal for the prize of the
upward call of God in Christ Jesus," and in Colossians 3:1-2, "If then
you have been raised with Christ, seek the things that are *above,* where
Christ is, seated at the right hand of God. Set your minds on things
that are *above,* not on things on the earth."

I even remembered some of the words of a poem whose author I
couldn't recall. Later I found the words by John Oxenham and recited
them in the sermon:

To every man there openeth a way and ways, and a way,
The high soul climbs the high way; The low soul gropes the low,
And, in between, on the misty flats, the rest drift to and fro,
And every man decideth, the way his soul shall go.[1]

The days of retreat on the lake flew by. I've never been an openly
pious person, but without a doubt those days were the occasion for
some of the most meaningful spiritual experiences of my life. I had
seldom before and have seldom since felt closer to the Lord or been
more aware of His leadership and inspiration. The sermon took shape,
at times the words coming almost like dictation, and as I prayed and
revised it, the final form focused on three themes, each addressing one
of the low points in the SBC odyssey: forced uniformity, political
coercion, and egotistic self-interest.

1. Let's turn from the misty flats of forced uniformity to the higher
   ground of autonomous individualism.
2. Let's turn from the muddy swamps of political coercion to the
   higher ground of spiritual persuasion.

3. Let's turn from the barren plains of egotistic self-interest to the higher ground of Christlike humility.

Back in Fort Worth, I asked Dean James McKinney of Southwestern's Music School to engage the talented faculty to prepare an uplifting arrangement of "Higher Ground" and to enlist the seminary's Men's Chorus to sing it just before I preached the sermon. I don't think I've ever heard a more rousing and inspiring rendition of this great hymn text. Anybody could have preached following that stirring message from the male voices of ministers called to serve the Lord through church music.

As the enthusiastic applause for the chorus began to die down and I made my way to the "see-through" Plexiglas^{TM} pulpit, I felt a sense of peace and assurance, and that was remarkable. Remarkable because when I was called to preach, there was one huge obstacle God had to help me overcome. It was a relentless case of severe shyness and stage fright. It was worse in my early days, diminished across years of experience, but it still persists. Even now, after fifty years of preaching, I never stand before a congregation without a sense of anxiety and nervousness. (As a teacher of preaching, I've indicated to students that it's probably better to have a little of that uneasiness than to be overly confident.) But on the platform at Kansas City before some 25,000 registered messengers, plus their families and visitors, my characteristic anxiety gave way to a sense of peaceful composure. It wasn't self-assurance, but the calm certainty that I wasn't alone and that the same God who had guided the preparation of the message was there to help me deliver it.

So, what better title and theme could I choose for this book than *Higher Ground: A Call to Christian Civility*? As I reflect on my involvement in Southern Baptist life, particularly during the last quarter century, I still believe it's important for all of us in the Baptist family and in the broader Christian family to hear the word of the Lord say again, "Set your minds on things that are above, not on things on the earth. . . . Seek the things that are above where Christ is. . . . Press on toward the goal for the prize of the upward call of God in Christ Jesus" (Col 3:1-2, Phil 3:14).

The plea of the book is expressed in the hymn text (with some minor liberties):

Lord, lift us up and help us stand,
By faith on Heaven's tableland;
A higher plane than we have found,
Lord, plant our feet on higher ground.

Note

[1] John Oxenham (William Arthur Dunkerley), "The Ways," in *Familiar Quotations*, ed. John Bartlett (Boston: Little, Brown & Co., 1955) 796.

Introduction

Friendly Fire

During my nine years in Atlanta, Georgia, where interest in the War Between the States (or the War of Northern Aggression as it was sometimes called) is still current, I learned about the military term "friendly fire." Even now, visiting one of the densely forested battlefields, one can imagine how it might have happened. The trees and underbrush are so thick that at times the soldiers couldn't tell if the approaching figures were friend or foe. It was not unusual for soldiers wearing both blue and gray to panic and fire through the woods only to discover they had wounded or killed their own comrades—hence the term "friendly fire."

During recent military action in Afghanistan and Iraq, there have been documented incidents of "friendly fire"—our military personnel mistakenly downing our own planes, destroying our own tanks, and accidentally shooting Iraqi policemen wrongly suspected of being insurgents.

The other kind of friendly fire, more difficult to comprehend, is the tactical decision to fire on one's own troops, intentionally risking the loss of the few for the good of the many. In World War II when enemy troops were closely engaged with Allied soldiers on the front lines, a painful decision was sometimes made to lay down an artillery barrage on the attacking enemy, knowing some Allied troops would also die in the process.

As I reflect on the carnage of the past quarter century of denominational strife in our Baptist family and remember how many have suffered not at the hands of the enemy, but as a result of the actions of fellow Baptists, the term "friendly fire" comes to mind. Some of it has been accidental; some has been intentional. When asked about such "collateral damage," one prominent leader of the SBC takeover party rationalized, "We knew we would have to break both arms of the Convention in order to save it."

Most people use the term "controversy" (defined as "a discussion of questions in which opposing opinions clash") to describe our denominational battles. But what fragmented our Baptist fellowship was something far more serious than that. It was a self-destructive, contentious, one-sided feud that at times took on combative characteristics. One Baptist leader spoke of it as a "holy war." Nevertheless, the term "controversy" is the euphemistic expression popularly employed to describe what happened, so I will use it too.

The Controversy

The "controversy" in the Southern Baptist Convention erupted the year I accepted the presidency of Southwestern Seminary. So in a way, my tenure, 1978–1994, paralleled the tragic family fight. Baptist disputes are nothing new; in fact, one might say criticism and opposition are a natural and expected experience for anyone engaged in an important enterprise.

In 1980, Dr. Peter Flawn, president of the University of Texas, invited me to preach at the university's baccalaureate service in Austin, Texas. We had dinner in his home, and he pointed to a framed statement hanging on the wall. It was a quote by Edmund Burke, the eighteenth-century English statesman. Since I was in the early years of my term as president of Southwestern Seminary, he thought I should be prepared for Burke's warning:

> Those who would carry on great public schemes must be proof against the worst fatiguing delays, the most mortifying disappointments, the most shocking insults, and what is worst of all, the presumptuous judgment of the ignorant upon their design.

That quote also found a place on my wall and in my experience at the seminary as well. But while this kind of opposition is to be expected, no one could have imagined that the initial harangues by a few outspoken fundamentalists in1978 about a supposed liberal drift in the SBC—particularly in the six Southern Baptist seminaries—would result in the fracturing of a great denomination. This controversy far exceeded any past disturbances both in extent, methodology, and outcome.

Concerns first surfaced at the news that a little-known Baptist judge named Paul Pressler and the head of a small Bible school named Paige Patterson, both Texans, were scheming to seize control of the denominational appointment process and ultimately the six seminaries and the entire Convention. Surely an effective denomination held together by the trust and voluntary cooperation of its 30,000 churches could not be so easily manipulated by two such unlikely individuals. And besides, experienced Baptists knew that the theological pendulum always seemed to return to the center after swinging back and forth between liberal views on the left and ultraconservative views on the right. There was an inherent natural corrective in our democratic structure that helped us avoid the ditches on either side of the road and kept our Convention centered where it belonged in the "radical middle."

But this assault on the Convention was different. The Patterson/Pressler coalition actually grabbed the free-swinging pendulum, forced it hard right, and held it there, disrupting the spontaneous corrective that had worked so effectively in the past. Admittedly, people dissatisfied with some action or trend would criticize, disrupt, and even boycott the Southern Baptist Convention, but no one had ever attempted—much less succeeded—in a takeover strategy to control its structure, organization, and operation.

Furthermore, the alarm clocks of concern went off at different times for different leaders, spreading out the effort to oppose the takeover and preventing a unified resistance. Looking back, had some of the tardy voices that eventually spoke out against the Patterson/Pressler league been raised earlier—in 1979 or 1980—the takeover could not have prevailed. I believe the mainstream majority, punctually aroused, would have turned back the assault in spite of all the underhanded political strategies the pair brazenly employed.

One of the depressing realizations of the early years of dissension was how many pastors, ministers, and lay leaders simply yearned to be on the winning side. Some lifted damp fingers into the air to detect which way the wind was blowing so they could safely go with the flow. For example, one pastor on the board at Southwestern Seminary rationalized to me his fundamentalist votes by saying, "I have to go along with them; they got me my church." If the tide had shifted away from the fundamentalists even once during the early years, these "go-with-the-winner-Baptists" (Pseudo-Baptists?) would have jumped quickly back to the majority side and assured victory for historic Baptists.

Another disappointment was the silence of some who disagreed with what was happening but were afraid to "stir up trouble" or risk losing friends or their church positions. As one religious reformer from the past said, "Silence is golden, but some silence is merely yellow."

U.S. Attorney General Robert F. Kennedy once warned Americans,

> Every time we turn our heads the other way when we see the law flouted—when we tolerate what we know to be wrong—when we close our eyes and ears to the corrupt because we are too busy, or too frightened—when we fail to speak up and speak out—we strike a blow against freedom and decency and justice.[1]

The closeness of the votes during the struggle for the SBC presidency supports the view that a few small variations could have made a difference and shifted the momentum back toward a traditional authentic Baptist Convention. For example, in 1988, when the Convention was held in San Antonio, fundamentalist Jerry Vines was elected over Richard Jackson by a slim majority of 692 votes out of 32,727 who attended. Only 347 messengers out of 32,000 shifting their votes would have defeated the takeover candidate. That same year, the SBC Woman's Missionary Union celebrated their one hundredth anniversary. They decided to hold their anniversary meeting in Richmond, Virginia, in May rather than during the Southern Baptist Convention in June when they typically met. Hundreds of women no doubt opted to go to Richmond and skip San Antonio that year. Since a large majority of the women in this mission organization would likely have voted for the traditional Baptist candidate, Richard Jackson, I believe the outcome would have been different.

That same year, when the vote was so close, I noticed that during the debates before the election of the president, several aggressive spokespeople representing the left of our Baptist spectrum made some contentious, intemperate remarks in support of women's ordination. The louder and longer they spoke, you could sense that some undecided messengers who were on the brink of voting against the takeover were frightened back across the line to vote for the fundamentalist candidate. If these overly zealous debaters had tempered the shock effect of their speeches, the vote might have been different.

Basically, Baptists are conservative in their theology and are fearful of anything that smacks of a liberal drift away from biblical principles. This hunger for maintaining sacred values probably caused some Baptists to vote for the fundamentalist agendas even though fundamentalism runs counter to their own ideals and interests.

It seemed that after the narrow defeat in 1988, opponents of the fundamentalist takeover began to lose heart, and never again were the votes that close. Eventually, "moderates," the uninspiring, gritless name sometimes given to those who resisted the Patterson/Pressler organization, either stopped attending the Convention meetings or gave up on organized efforts to defeat the takeover efforts.

One of the inevitable outcomes of the coarsening of our denominational meetings and the rude acrimony that has characterized our debates is the reluctance of sensitive well-mannered people to participate. Rather than getting sucked up in the rancorous wrangling, they quietly drop out, and the quality of the participation is thereby diminished. The discussions are left in the hands of mean-spirited extremists.

In many respects, the fundamentalist attack was not just against the structure and organization of the Convention; it was an attack on the spirit of our Baptist family, the positive spirit of fellowship, the spirit of trust, civility, and cooperation. Since the Southern Baptist Convention was held together by the fragile bond of voluntary cooperation, and since voluntary cooperation depends on trust, the destruction of that spirit spelled the eventual demise of voluntary cooperancy.

Since 1992, the fundamentalist candidates for SBC president have been basically unopposed, signaling the fact that the hardliners have achieved total "victory" by squelching any contrary voices and basically purging all disagreement. The great Southern Baptist Convention has been in the hands of "alien" Baptists and, in my opinion, will never return to its former glory.

The Way Forward: Higher Ground

How then, shall divided Baptists, as well as other Christian groups weighed down by a recent history of controversy, move forward, leaving unfortunate fractures behind, and press on to higher ground? The hymn expresses the prayer and aim of this book:

> My heart has no desire to stay,
> Where doubts arise and fears dismay;
> Though some may dwell where these abound,
> My prayer, my aim is higher ground.

We must not dwell on the past twenty-five years, but neither should we carelessly discount them nor forget both the wrongdoings of those who assaulted the Convention and the sometimes embarrassing failures among those of us who opposed them. We need to reflect on the bad things and learn from them. Billy Sunday claimed that ignoring history and forgetting its lessons is dangerous. He warned that passing time has a way of erasing the seriousness of wrongdoing, quelling our sense of outrage, and encouraging apathy:

> Events rot away like corpses, their traces ever fainter in the earth, the fingerprints of the sinner ever more difficult to detect. Until all that's left are the faint stains of outrage which surround the sites of crimes.[2]

So the best way forward from this quarter century of strife is to let the past convict us and work to restore a gentler, kinder tone in our discourse and deliberations—in short—a return to Christian civility. That's the road to higher ground.

For example, looking back, we need to acknowledge the stinging indictment leveled at Baptists in the South by some of our critics. They accuse Baptists of being proud, self-sufficient, and even triumphalistic in our progress and growth. There is truth in that accusation. At times we Baptists boastfully considered ourselves not only the largest non-Roman Catholic denomination in the country, but the best. As one Alabama Baptist preacher expressed it, "Southern Baptists are God's last hope…His only hope for evangelizing this world."[3] In more recent years, a former Southern Baptist Convention president, admitting that it sounded like megalomania, made a similar exaggerated claim,

> I believe that the hope of the world lies in the West. I believe the hope of the West lies in America. I believe the hope of America is in Judeo-Christian ethics. I believe that the backbone of that Judeo-Christian ethic is evangelical Christianity. I believe that the bellwether of evangelical Christianity is the Southern Baptist Convention. So I believe, in a sense, that as the Southern Baptist Convention goes, so goes the world.[4]

Texas Baptists recently made a similar blunder in their bold claims about their mission outreach in the Minnesota-Wisconsin area, inaccurately boasting that we Texans "launched" Baptist work in those two states. The implication was that until Texas Baptists came to the rescue, Minnesota and Wisconsin were bereft of evangelical witness among a population that was "religious but with no personal experience with Christ."

Roger Olson, who joined the faculty at Baylor's Truett Seminary from Bethel Seminary in Minnesota, wrote the following correction in a letter to the *Baptist Standard:*

As a native Midwesterner, I would like to correct some misinformation in the article "Texas Baptists connected by family ties to churches in Minnesota-Wisconsin Convention" (Sept. 20, 2004).

It states, "Texas Baptists were integral in launching Baptist ministry in Minnesota and Wisconsin 50 years ago, as Texas pastors and laypeople movd north to start the initial Baptist churches in the region."

In fact, Baptists have been alive and well in the region for well over 150 years and did not come from the South.

The article also states that "less than 5 percent of people (in Minnesota and Wisconsin) are evangelical Christians." The Evangelical Covenant Church of America is the seventh-largest denomination in Minnesota and has churches throughout Wisconsin. The Evangelical Free Church of America is also very pervasive in both states. There is a large and active Greater Minnesota Association of Evangelicals that sponsors evangelical activities throughout the state. I am confident many more than 5 percent are Evangelical.

Finally, the article closes by implying that people in Minnesota and Wisconsin are religious but do not have a personal relationship with Jesus. While these two states are not part of the traditional "Bible Belt," many of the people there are born-again Christians and experienced personal relationship with Jesus without ever meeting a Southern Baptist.

I applaud the work of the Minnesota-Wisconsin Baptist Convention but urge them to acknowledge the presence of other Evangelicals and Baptists doing kingdom work in my home state and its neighbor state.[5]

This tendency toward uncouth denominational smugness has sometimes made us impervious to corrective criticism. As Tocqueville warned, when one lives "in a state of perpetual self-adoration, only past experience is able to bring certain truths to our attention."[6] Now, as a result of the controversy with its failures from both the right and the left, we've been brought down a notch. Our denominational effectiveness has been seriously eroded. Our best hope for redeeming that past is to learn from it. Patrick Henry said it well: "We have but one lamp by which our feet are guided; and that is the lamp of experience."[7]

The purpose of this book is not merely to point out what's wrong or to cast stones at expressions of incivility. In fact, each chapter offers a "higher ground" alternative. The book is an attempt to shine the lamp of experience on our history and let it guide Baptists and other believers to take the higher ground: a place defined as the gracious, restrained, and well-mannered disposition of Christian civility.

Notes

[1] Robert F. Kennedy, *A New Day: Robert F. Kennedy* (New York: New American Library, 1968) 26.

[2] Quoted in *USA Today,* 27 June 1996, D9.

[3] Bill J. Leonard, *God's Last & Only Hope* (Grand Rapids: Eerdmans, 1990) 2.

[4] Adrian Rogers quoted in "No Comment Department," *Christian Century* 109/26 (9-16 September 1992): 796.

[5] Roger E. Olson, "Texas Baptist Forum," *Baptist Standard* (1 October 2004) 5.

[6] Alexis de Tocqueville, *Democracy in America* (New York: D. Appleton Co., 1899) 282.

[7] William Wirt, *Sketches of the Life and Character of Patrick Henry:* (Philadelphia: James Webster, 1836) 138.

Christian Civility, Not Rancor

The Need for National Civility

"America is spiraling into a cesspool of political vitriol."

"Political discourse has been replaced by polarization, personal attacks, and blind partisanship."

"We live in an uncouth, coarse, and bad-mannered era."

"Rudeness is rising, crassness is increasing in all regions of America according to a new survey."

"A rancorous environment awash in disagreement and division has led to a multitude of Americans moving to Mexico."

These headlines from recent media articles condemning the coarsening tone of public discourse in our country point to a growing outcry for civility in our national life. Even as I sat down to write this paragraph, I glanced at a front-page article in the morning paper by journalist Jacquielynn Floyd. She was rightly concerned that much of the debate about the Iraq war is dominated by vitriolic extremists. The discussion is "being co-opted by shrill, angry rhetoric from both ends of the political spectrum. Polarized political warfare between all-or-nothing extremists is disheartening and ultimately unproductive. ...People are discouraged by all the screaming and vitriol." What we need, she suggested, is reasoned, informed debate.[1]

The same concerns were cited in a two-year study among representative adults by the research organization called Public Agenda. It shows that Americans are intensely frustrated by the pushy rudeness and lack of respect they increasingly encounter in their daily lives. Unhappiness with "reckless drivers, cell-phone abuse, poor customer service, swearing, and litter" came from all segments of our culture—big cities, small towns, north, south, rich and poor. According to the survey, 6 in 10 Americans believe this coarseness is getting worse, 79 percent say "lack of respect and courtesy has become a serious national problem," and 73 percent percent believe that in the past, citizens treated one another with greater respect.[2]

Furthermore, this collapse of civility is not just an American crisis. British writer Lynne Truss, bestselling author of *Eats, Shoots and Leaves*, a zero-tolerance approach to grammar and punctuation, has taken on what she calls the utter rudeness of the world today. Her new book, *Talk to the Hand*, decries the boorish behavior and the sorry state of modern manners in the United Kingdom. The title is taken from an often repeated expression on the *Jerry Springer Show* when an angry participant tries to silence opposition by holding out an aggressive palm at arm's length and saying, "Talk to the hand 'cause the face ain't listening!" In her rallying cry for civility, Truss attributes the situation to "A lazy moral relativism combined with aggressive social insolence."[3]

Is this loss of a civil tone in public life that serious? Has our twenty-first-century culture really becoming a "spiraling cesspool of vitriolic behavior"? Journalist Edwin Feulner believes it is. He claims the worsening can be explained in part by what he calls the "broken-window theory." When a broken window in a deserted building is left unrepaired, the rest of the windows will soon be broken by vandals. If one person scrawls graffiti on a wall, others will soon be at it with their spray cans. Feulner believes today's disturbing growth of incivility follows and confirms this "broken-window theory." Let a few belligerent leaders from either side of a debate introduce mean-spirited, sledgehammer attacks on their opponents, and sure enough, "further down the food chain, lesser lights will take up smaller hammers and commit even more degrading incivilities."[4] Once someone wields the hammer—once the incivility starts—others join in, and pretty soon it's no longer a debate. It's a back-alley brawl.

So the loss of civility is not just a social blunder to be compared with using the wrong fork at the dinner table. Rather, it's a grave threat to the basic fabric of our democratic society. Lord Radcliffe called this witless rejection of civility "the Black Death of the twentieth century." [5]

It's no wonder then that we're hearing widespread pleas for a softening of public discourse and calls for a resurgence of civility in public life. They appear in a rash of new books on the subject: Leroy Rouner's *Civility,* Richard Mouw's *Uncommon Decency,* Stephen Carter's *Civility: Manners, Morals, and the Etiquette of Democracy,* and P. M. Forni's *Choosing Civility* are examples. (Thirty books and a dozen articles are listed in the bibliographies at the end of this book.) Furthermore, the Civility Initiative at Johns Hopkins University is one of several recent educational programs focusing on the academic study of civility in contemporary society.

Civility in this public context can be defined as a code of behavior based on respect, restraint, and consideration. It's a kind of gracious statesmanship that includes courtesy, politeness, and good manners. Students in a university class on civility cited the following additional characteristics: kindness, tolerance, tact, moderation, grace, charm, and empathy.

Civility is public politeness, tact, moderation, and good manners even toward people who are different and with whom we disagree on important matters. Instead of trashing and demonizing those who differ, civility hears their positions with decorum and grace and then politely answers their views with reasoned substance and informed opinion. In a word, civility is kindness. Henry James once said, "Three things in human life are important; the first is to be kind, the second is to be kind, and the third is to be kind."[6]

The dictionary definition is

Civility n., pl. –ties [ME. <Ofr. *civilien* < L. *civilitas* (< *civilis,* civil), politics, hence politic behavior, politeness] 1. Courteous behavior, politeness, acting in accordance with organized society, observing accepted social usages, not rude. Humane, ethical, reasonable, refined, cultured, polished.

In its simplest form, civility means niceness. In some ways it is personified in the old-fashioned concept of "the gentleman." "The gentleman" relates to others with dignity, honor, and gallantry. It's expressed in the old idea of chivalry, defending the weak and the endangered at personal risk.

Abraham Lincoln's sage advice is apropos: practice "malice toward none and charity for all" because "a house divided against itself cannot stand." This kind of common civility that encourages reasoned discourse without rancor is indispensable to the exchange of ideas in a free society. That's why our Declaration of Independence calls for a "decent respect for the opinions of mankind." That in itself would be ample justification for a campaign to restore civility to public life.

The Need for Christian Civility

But while improving the tenor of public civility is important, this book calls for a distinctive form of Christian civility defined by qualities of Christlikeness. It's a modest plea for Christians to practice in our religious and denominational dialogues a civil behavior guided by biblical principles. Christian civility includes all the definitive terms of ordinary civility discussed above, but it is further refined by such biblical principles as the golden rule, the fruit of the Spirit, and the example of Jesus. The purpose of this book is to call us to the higher ground of *Christian* civility.

Tragically, the culture of public coarseness has invaded our church and denominational life. In a recent *Newsweek* article on spirituality, Martin Marty decries the changes he sees in religious dialogue in twenty-first-century America: "If the mid-century revival represented an era of spiritual *good* feelings, in the new millennium *ill* feelings test the hospitable spirit that should characterize the religious quest."[7]

Those "ill feelings" have been embarrassingly prevalent in the recent denominational controversy among Baptists. I'm not sure which came first, but the same uncivilized tone so typical in our national discourse has infected our Baptist family as well. During the twenty-five-year internecine struggle for the future of the Southern Baptist Convention, the tenor of our debates has coarsened. When fundamentalists organized a political effort to gain control of the Convention in order to reshape it according to their perspectives, they opened the door for a mean-spirited mindset of caustic polarization.

Ironically, one of the historic hallmarks of Baptist identity has been our respect for individual freedom and autonomy. Expressed in the principle called "the priesthood of the believer," this unique hallmark espouses the sacred right of each believer to respond to God through Christ according to conscience without interference from any human authority. The *Baptist Faith and Message* explains,

> Baptists emphasize the soul's competency before God, freedom in religion, and the priesthood of the believer. However, this emphasis should not be interpreted to mean that there is an absence of certain definite doctrines that Baptists believe, cherish, and with which they have been and are now closely identified.[8]

So while there are basic beliefs that we share together under the banner of Baptist principles, and while we've from time to time defined what it means to be a Baptist, we've traditionally allowed for diversity within the broad tenets of our faith and have encouraged reasoned dialogue among fellow believers. At our best, when Baptists have disagreed we've disagreed agreeably, respecting each other's convictions and humbly and honestly evaluating our positions in the light of Scripture. As long as we remained within the basic parameters of generally accepted Baptist beliefs, we were free to hold diverse viewpoints. We still remained colleagues, sisters and brothers in the same family.

But during these past twenty-five years, instead of being at our best, the Baptist family began to mimic the harsh strategies of secular politicians, and we revealed our worst side. We've become a denomination at each other's throats. Along with "road rage," "air rage," and "sports rage" (Out-of-control parents are now required to enroll in workshops on civil cheering!), we're now faced with "church rage" and "denominational rage."

It's become almost routine in Baptist deliberations and publications for ministers and lay leaders to employ rude distortions, exaggerations, insinuations, unsubstantiated accusations, and outright misrepresentations in order to slander and demonize opponents. Someone who votes a certain way or holds a certain position is quickly condemned—not just for lack of judgment or knowledge, but for being "liberal" or "extremist" or even for being "a godless infidel." We've made an art form out of branding our opponents with derogatory labels.

After fundamentalist leaders in the Southern Baptist Convention broke their century-old tie with more than 200 groups connected through the Baptist World Alliance, a secular newspaper reporter asked, "Why do Southern Baptists have this scorched-earth approach to everything?" Unfortunately, that self-righteous exclusivism has become the widely accepted impression of Southern Baptists held by many observers of our denomination.

Instead of processing our disagreements with a constructive exchange of ideas that listens respectfully to the other side, too many take the shortcut of condemning and belittling their opponents. Calling those who disagree "wicked" is usually an excuse for avoiding reasoned debate on real issues, and it's a lot easier than trying to convince them or hearing their attempts to convince us.

A Wiley Miller cartoon shows a hapless man saying, "Of course, that's just my opinion." In response, he is screamed at by a purse-whacking woman who knocks him to the ground. Prostrate, he feebly inquires, "Whatever happened to 'I respectfully disagree'?"[9] It used to be common in polite debates to hear a speaker refer to the other side as "my worthy opponent." I haven't heard that expression lately.

Christian Civility Is a Biblical Mandate

Self-righteous demagoguery with its shouting, name-calling, and derision should have no place among those committed to the authority of the Bible that teaches the opposite. In fact, civility is the least that can

ˑsus Christ. The least we can do

ˑration, and kindness to the

ˑhe Lord Jesus Christ are

expeˑ   ot just ordinary civility

but a "supˑ   ˑ spirituality, godli-

ness, and Chrisˑ   ˑ be

consistent with the claim that wˑ   ˑy

grace, and that we're followers of the Son ˑ

While civility is not a biblical term as sucˑˑ,

Listen to the clear teachings of the word of God:

- Pursue peace with everyone. (Heb 12:14)
- Speak evil of no one, avoid quarreling, be gentle, and show every courtesy to everyone. (Titus 3:2)
- Conduct yourselves wisely toward outsiders. . . . Let your speech always be gracious, [with gracious charm]. (Col 4:5-6)
- Avoid disputing about words, which does no good, but only ruins the hearers . . . avoid Godless chatter . . . . Have nothing to do with stupid, senseless controversies; you know that they breed quarrels, and the Lord's servant must not be quarrelsome, but kindly to everyone . . . forbearing, gentle. (2 Tim 2:14, 16, 23-26)
- Through love be servants of one another. For the whole law is fulfilled in one word, 'You shall love your neighbor as yourself.' But if you bite and devour one another, take heed that you are not consumed by one another. . . . The fruit (harvest) of the Spirit is love joy, peace, patience, kindness, goodness, faithfulness, gentleness, self-control. . . . Let us have no self-conceit, no provoking of one another, no envy of one another. (Gal 5:13-25)
- Love is patient and kind; love is not jealous or boastful; it's not arrogant or rude. Love does not insist on its own way; it's not irritable or resentful; it does not rejoice at wrong, but rejoices in the right. Love bears all things, believes all things, hopes all things, endures all things. (1 Cor 13:4-7)
- I Paul, myself, entreat you by the meekness and gentleness of Christ . . . that though we live in the world we are not carrying on a worldly war, for the weapons of our warfare are not worldly but have divine power. (2 Cor 10:1, 3-4)

- Always be ready to make a defense to anyone who calls you to account for the hope that is in you, yet do it with gentleness and reverence. (1 Pet 3:15)
- If it's possible, so far as it depends on you, live peaceably with all. (Rom 12:18)
- Let every man be quick to hear, slow to speak, slow to anger. (Jas 1:19)
- We also have the unequivocal command from God to love our neighbor as ourselves. (Matt 22:39)

Not only is it clearly expressed in writing, but we have the preeminent example of this high brand of civility in our Lord Himself. He had all power, but He came in the form of a servant; He came in love. He endured the weakness and vulnerability of the cross. Jesus was slow to anger, abounding in love and faithfulness. He possessed omnipotence, but He served with kindness and gentleness. That's why one of our favorite hymns proclaims, "softly and tenderly Jesus is calling." Our Lord requires no less of us, His followers.

Along with all this, Christians have experienced the forgiving grace of Almighty God who has the power to judge and condemn, but that all-powerful God deals with us in loving kindness. That means that we Christians should have a civility advantage over most people.

Christian Civility Does Not Mean Giving up Convictions

In trying to explain why the SBC leaders decided to separate from their Baptist sisters and brothers in the Baptist World Alliance (BWA), John Pierce, editor of the Baptist news journal *Baptists Today*, wrote,

> Southern Baptist leaders first made it clear they will not cooperate in missions and ministry with anyone who does not fully embrace their ever-narrowing theology and heavy-handed methodologies. Now we know they are not interested in even talking with other Christians either—including fellow Baptists. . . . For current Southern Baptist leaders, cooperation and conversation are wrongly equated with compromising convictions. [10]

But Christian civil... ...it doesn't require us to water down beliefs to some toothless low common denominator. It merely calls for a polite respect for the conscience of others, a willingness to listen to differing points of view. Civility doesn't threaten orthodoxy; it simply recognizes that others have a right to look at things differently, and that when they share their views with us they can expect a fair hearing. "The issue is not whether to stand firm or compromise, but how to express our firmness. We need to learn how to be sensitive and assertive at the same time with seriousness of intent and lightness of touch."[11]

But when all potential sources of dissent are removed from the conversation—as they were for example when the SBC separated itself from the BWA—productive dialogue is squelched, and the atmosphere in which constructive and wise decisions can be made is poisoned.

Martin Marty had a point when he observed that the people who are good at being civil often lack strong convictions and people who have strong convictions often lack civility. But our Christian faith teaches us to do both: to hold on to our principles while at the same time tolerating and respecting those with whom we disagree. We're to respect them as human beings created in the divine image. Richard Mouw put it convincingly: "Civility and firm resolve can live easily with one another. Our challenge is to come up with a 'convicted civility.'"[12]

This relationship between a civil spirit and a commitment to convictions is expressed clearly by the Apostle Peter; "Always be ready to make your defense for the hope that is in you," he instructed. But then he added, "Yet do it with gentleness and reverence." (1 Pet 3:15-16)

Christian Civility Does Not Mean Giving up Strong Provocative Language

The Bible makes it clear that speech is a powerful and at times even dangerous commodity and that Christians should guard their tongues. "Sticks and stones may break my bones, but words will never hurt me" isn't really true. Words can hurt. They can degrade, discourage, and inflame.

When television evangelist Pat Robertson called for the assassination of a South American dictator because it would be cheaper and would not interfere with the exporting of oil to the United States, his language was not only un-Christian; it was dangerous. Verbal violence can quickly lead to physical violence because "language is the womb of action."[13]

But the dangerous potential of speech should not cause Christians to become timid or inarticulate when we speak our convictions. We should not, in the name of civility, give up colorful, forceful speech for bland, politically correct language that's dull and tiresome. Paul advised early Christians to let their speech be "seasoned with salt" (Col 4:6). He was suggesting that our conversation about Jesus ought to have the salty tang of forceful, genuine experience. Our words ought to be real and persuasive. As one commentator described,

> Vigorous and passionate debate helps us to define issues and to sharpen positions. However, when debates about policies and ideas devolve into attacks on individuals, we lose the chance for civil and productive dialogue and achieving real social justice.[14]

The Lord Jesus, our perfect example of civility, often used terse, provocative language, particularly when He was opposing evil. He condemned the self-righteousness of the Pharisees with surprising abruptness. They were acting like "serpents" (Matt 23:33), "vipers (Matt 3:7), "hypocrites" (Matt 23:14), and "whitewashed tombs" (Matt 23:27). Even though He had the authority to judge their actions, and even though He spoke plainly, Jesus never stooped to profane or vulgar language. He maintained a civil spirit, condemning the sin rather than the individual.

What Christian civility rejects is demeaning and disrespectful attacks on those with whom we disagree. While respecting the other person's dignity and worth in the eyes of God—even those who are strangers—we can still use strong persuasive language. But there is no cause to be rude. Eric Hoffman said, "Rudeness is the weak man's imitation of strength."[15]

In his book on civility, Stephen L. Carter warned that abusive language not only demeans the speaker and violates common morality, but it also hurts our democratic social order. Cleansing our language of violence is not simply a matter of politeness—it's a matter of morality. And, at a practical level, it's a matter of making conversation work. Nasty language, whether vulgar or violent or simply bigoted, does nothing to encourage a thoughtful and reasoned response. It sparks anger or shame but not dialogue. So it makes it harder for us to talk to each other and thus hurts democracy.[16]

Christian Civility Does Not Mean Giving up Witnessing or Evangelizing Others

Admittedly, some of us are reluctant when it comes to sharing our faith or trying to convince a non-Christian to become a believer. Afraid of overreaching, becoming pushy, or intruding inappropriately in another person's life, we sometimes remain silent. Maybe it's because we've seen so many embarrassing examples of intrusive witnessing—lapel-grabbing, in-your-face, Bible-thumping, pompous witnessing—and we decide we want no part in that.

But at the heart of our Christian faith is the central belief that there's only one way for sinful humanity to be reconciled to God, to be forgiven and redeemed for all eternity. We believe with all our hearts that we're saved only when we accept God's free gift of salvation through personal faith in the Lord Jesus Christ. Since that is such an unequivocal doctrine, and since we believe it whole-heartedly, then it would be unloving, unforgivable, and even uncivil not to propagate that good news. Besides that, God commands us to go and tell. Even though it's not easy, and even though it may appear intrusive and embarrassing, there's no excuse for dodging the responsibility.

The challenge is finding the appropriate civil way to do it. In some situations, the appropriate method involves direct, bold approaches to strangers. But some of the best opportunities to witness appear indirectly, serendipitously. If we're alert and sensitive, we'll take advantage of these golden opportunities that come our way. It may be in the middle of a telephone call, during an unexpected conversation with an acquaintance, at the point of a despised interruption, or at the time of a chance encounter. Our ears need to be programmed to pick up on these unplanned occasions when the door is opened to tell someone else what Jesus means to us and how they can have the same experience. The Apostle Paul obviously understood this. Listen to his inspired advice: "Conduct yourselves wisely toward outsiders [unbelievers], making the most of every opportunity" (Col 4:5).

There are other times when our witness can be best shared after a long process of building friendships and trust with unbelievers. We call this "lifestyle evangelism." Still other situations open up when personal needs have been met, an act of kindness rendered, or a service provided. Missionaries in foreign cultures have long understood that lost people are more responsive to the gospel when the missionaries have provided schools, hospitals, clothing, and food for needy people.

Success in other situations comes only after an extended time of friendly, civil dialogue with those of other faiths. This is especially true when Christians try to share their faith with Jews. The long history of anti-Semitism—often under the Christian banner—makes witnessing to Jews especially sensitive. No matter how essential and true we believe our gospel to be and no matter how loving our intentions, one can understand why Jewish people might consider our witnessing to be a hostile act.

That's why Baptists in recent years decided to initiate dialogue sessions, "conversations" between Baptists and Jews. These were designed to foster understanding of each other's convictions, but they also offered opportunities to share our Christian faith with Jewish participants in a non-hostile environment. These planned conversations were not "easy substitutes" for the harder task of personal evangelism. They didn't, as some critics suggest, imply that the participants believed all religions are equally true. They don't imply that dialogues are all we need to do to obey the command to "make disciples of all nations." But they were effective attempts to do what Paul suggested: "Conduct yourselves wisely toward outsiders" (Col 4:5).

During the seventies and eighties, the Southern Baptist Home Mission Board sponsored some productive interfaith conversations with American Jewish representatives. Doors of trust and inquiry were opened. As suspicions diminished, participants opened up, and more accurate understandings of both Christian and Jewish doctrines resulted. Who knows what opportunities for evangelism would have resulted had the conversations continued? But one thoughtless public remark from a fundamentalist president of the SBC disrupted this process and eventually wiped out the progress that had been made.

In 1980, Bailey Smith said, "God Almighty does not hear the prayer of a Jew." Not only did that comment stifle a healthy interfaith dialogue and embarrass Baptists before the world, it also generated an upheaval within the SBC that some believe furthered the tragic controversy that divided our Baptist family.[18] On the heels of his remark, the new fundamentalist leaders of the Southern Baptist Convention went on to trash the healthy dialogues, calling them "pathetic," and have now replaced them with official Convention resolutions crudely "targeting" Jewish people for direct proselytizing. They have proposed prayer campaigns for Jewish salvation that are insensitively scheduled to coincide with Judaism's High Holy Days.

Christian civility doesn't mean giving up witnessing or adopting universalism's claim that all religions are equal and that everybody will eventually be saved. Instead, Christian civility calls for courageous witnesses who will boldly share their faith in a congenial, gracious, Christlike spirit that will draw unbelievers to Jesus rather than drive them away. Jesus Himself obviously had such a pleasant, approachable personality. Prodigals felt comfortable coming to Him. They believed He would understand them and receive them lovingly. Little children don't flock around cranky unpleasant scolders, but they rushed to be around Jesus.

That led the Apostle Paul to urge first-century believers to share their faith in a pleasant, appealing manner. In his letter to the Colossian church, he asked them to pray that God would help him be an effective witness in prison:

Pray for us that God may open to us a door for the word, to declare the mystery of Christ, on account of which I am in prison, that I may make it clear, as I ought to speak. (Col 4:3-4)

He then gave those first-century Christians a brief lesson in how to witness bravely, but in a civil, thoughtful, sensitive manner:

Conduct yourselves wisely toward outsiders. . . . Let your speech always be gracious, seasoned with salt, so that you may know how you ought to answer every one. (Col 4:5-6)

I saw a bumper sticker the other day that said, "Have you noticed how many born again people make you wish they hadn't been born the first time?" That's a terrible indictment! When we show Christ to others, we ought to be so gracious, so genial, so winsome that we draw people to Him. We have a stewardship of personality, and we'll be accountable for that stewardship someday. Did you offend people, did you push them away, or did you draw people to the Lord by your witness? Christian civility calls for bold witnessing that draws people to Jesus.

Christian Civility Is Perfectly Expressed in Agape Love

With remarkable uniformity, the Bible gives the concept of *agape* love a supreme position. Whenever it points to what is highest, greatest, or best—whenever it identifies superlatives—it points to love.

For example, our Lord Himself spoke of love as the greatest commandment of all. In 1 Peter 4, Simon Peter wrote, "Above all things, have love among yourselves." In Romans 13 and Galatians 5, Paul said, "Love is the fulfillment of all the law . . . the greatest of these is love." And in his Gospel, John gave us the mother of all précis: "God is love." In the Bible, love is the *summum bonum,* the irreducible essential, the encapsulation of the faith.

To understand how such an exalted position could be given to this one theme, you have to understand the true biblical meaning of love.

Agape love is not a feeling or emotion. It's not a romantic, physical attraction. It's not the warm affection we have for family and close friends. *Agape* is a sturdy word, not mushy or blurred. It involves an attitude chosen by an act of will. It's an intentional outlook of unselfish concern you take toward someone else. *Agape* is an outgoing mindset of unconquerable benevolence you choose to take toward others in society. Nothing another person does can keep you from wishing for them the very best.

In fact, the King James Version translates *agape* as "charity." "Now abides faith, hope, and charity" (1 Cor 13:13). Charity conveys the idea of action. I have a book whose title expresses that idea, *Love Is Something You Do*. *Agape* is radical love, Good Samaritan love, and when we understand love in this way it helps clarify a troubling commandment. God orders us to love our enemies. If loving my enemies means gritting my teeth and working up a warm feeling of affection toward people I don't even like, it's an impossible command. We can't generate toward our enemies the same kind of loving affection we have for our family and friends. We don't command our feelings and emotions that way. But if loving people in the biblical sense means intentionally choosing an attitude toward them of unselfish concern, then with God's help I can obey that command.

That kind of open, outward, unselfish viewpoint toward others captures the essence of Christian civility. It's more than being nice. It's not just play-acting, hypocritically masking our hostile feelings with polite words and grudging accommodation. Instead, it's actively putting yourself in another's place. It's acting toward them in the same way you would want them to act toward you—with respect, decency, consideration, and kindness. It's choosing deliberately to put into practice what the Bible says is the greatest thing in the world: *agape* love. What better definition of Christian civility could there be?

The rest of this book is an attempt to show what it means to claim the higher ground of Christian civility in diverse areas of daily life.

Notes

[1] Jacquielynn Floyd, "We Need Reasoned Debate," *Dallas Morning News,* 23 August 2005, B1.

[2] "Aggravating Circumstances: A Status Report on Rudeness in America," *Public Agenda,* <www.publicagenda.org> (2005).

[3] Lynn Truss, *Talk to the Hand* (New York: Gotham Books, 2005) 6.

[4] Edwin Feulner, "Civility Smash Test," *Dallas Morning News,* 22 May 2005. C1

[5] "Censorship," *Encyclopaedia Britannica* (24 August, 2005) <www.britannica.com/eb/article-14938>.

[6] P. M. Forni, *Choosing Civility* (New York: St. Martin's Griffin, 2002), 3. Author quotes Henry James.

[7] Martin Marty, "The Long and Winding Road," *Newsweek* (29 August 2005): 65.

[8] Herschel Hobbs, *The Baptist Faith and Message,* (Nashville: Convention Press, 1971) 4.

[9] Abigail McCarthy, "Mind Your Manners," *Commonweal* (21 May 1999): 8.

[10] John D. Pierce, "Cooperation," *Baptists Today* (February 2005): 7.

[11] P. M. Forni, *Choosing Civility,* 25.

[12] Richard J. Mouw, *Uncommon Decency,* (Downers Grove: InterVarsity Press, 1992) 12.

[13] Ibid., 44.

[14] Andrew Sandlin, "Civility in Discourse," <www.*Razormouth.com*> (26 July 2002).

[15] "Civility in Public Discourse," *The Interfaith Alliance,* <http//www.interfaithalliance.org>.

[16] Forni, *Choosing Civility,* 22.

[17] Stephen L. Carter, *Civility: Manners, Morals, and the Etiquette of Democracy* (New York: Basic Books, 1998) 151.

[18] Daniel E. Goodman, "Baptist Leader's Divisive 1980 Remark Helped Launch a Conservative Revolution," *Dallas Morning News,* 3 September 2005, G4.

Biblical Obedience,
Not Biblical Defense

By their own account, when the architects of the fundamentalist takeover of the Southern Baptist Convention explored various "hot-button" issues around which they could rally support for their cause, they finally settled on one. They would marshal their followers to rise up and defend the Bible. They also chose the term "inerrant" as the only acceptable term to express the trustworthiness of the Bible. That term provided a simplistic yardstick for testing loyalty to their party. Those who were willing to say, "I believe the Bible is inerrant" passed the test. Those who for one reason or another did not like the term "inerrant" failed the test, even if they held an equally orthodox view of the absolute trustworthiness and authority of Scripture. At times, the difference between the "ins" and the "outs" was purely semantic, not substantive.

As it turned out, the "inerrancy party" spent enormous amounts of time and energy defending the Bible, not against unbelievers who rejected it as God's inspired word, but against fellow believers who simply preferred other language to express their absolute confidence in the truth and authority of Scripture. During the early years of the controversy, I regularly received letters as seminary president asking me to require all the faculty of the seminary to declare their belief in the "inerrancy" of Scripture. I would explain that they had already confirmed their commitment to the Bible by endorsing the strong statement on Scripture in *The Baptist Faith and Message* that included the wording "It is a perfect treasure of divine instruction. It has God for its author, salvation for its end, and truth, without any mixture of error, for its matter." But that never seemed to be sufficient.

Frequently someone would respond, "I know they believe it, but can't you just get them to say, 'I believe it's inerrant'?"

Based in part on this kind of faulty reasoning, the fundamentalist leaders claimed that the SBC seminaries were harboring liberal professors who did not believe the Bible. However, from among the more than 400 teachers at the time, they could name fewer than a dozen whose "liberalism" was composed of more than merely a refusal to use inerrancy terminology. And even among those few examples, not one held classical liberal views denouncing the Bible as the inspired, authoritative word of God. The examples of their "liberalism" were usually matters of interpretation with which the fundamentalists disagreed.

There were some of those accused who did indeed hold interpretations that differed from traditional Baptist views. But, in some cases, the people cited had already been addressed. Some of them no longer taught in one of our schools. Others were on the faculties of Baptist universities, not seminaries. Finally, after all these exceptions, there were a small number within the dozen whose positions were outside the parameters of what Baptists would expect of seminary teachers, and they should have been corrected.

Admittedly, our six theological seminaries were not perfect. Since the faculty and administration of these institutions were fallible human beings, there were, and there would always be, some who fell short of expectations. As president of Southwestern Seminary in Fort Worth, Texas, one of my responsibilities was to monitor carefully the performance of 150 faculty members, 50 administrative staff members, and more than 200 employees and part-time workers. We all were expected to live up to the highest standards of moral behavior as well as the theological guidelines of *The Baptist Faith and Message*.

Unfortunately, it became necessary during my sixteen years as president to dismiss or request the resignation of about a dozen teachers and an equal number of staff members. At other times, less serious disciplinary action was required. These corrective steps were carried out quietly, redemptively, and (with rare exceptions) without sensational headlines. Over the sixteen years, these rare examples constituted a very small minority.

The point is that while there were (and always will be) seminary personnel who fail to live up to the standards, Southwestern, and I am confident the other seminaries as well, dealt with them quickly and appropriately, and, in my opinion, were doing a commendable job of maintaining high levels of faithfulness to our denominational expectations. The accusations of theological liberalism had no substantive basis, and they certainly did not justify the tragic disruption of a large and effective denomination.

Sadly, the wrangling within the Baptist family largely degenerated into an inane contest among Bible believers over who could express their convictions with the most sensational flare. "I believe the Bible from cover to cover!" "That's nothing. I believe every word in every sentence!" "I believe the Bible is absolutely inerrant!" "Oh, but I believe it is supremely, infallibly inerrant." "I'm ahead of all of you. I even believe the notes and maps in the back of the Bible!"

All that energy and enthusiasm should have been aimed at obeying the Bible rather than scrambling to defend it. Paul encouraged the Roman Christians to "outdo one another in showing honor" (Rom 12:10, NIV). Maybe we could add that believers should "outdo one another in putting the Bible into practice!" The Bible says, "Be doers of the word, and not hearers only, deceiving yourselves" (Jas 1:22).

To be sure, those of us who believe that the Bible is the miraculous word of God have found it necessary from time to time to confront agnostics who belittle it as "just another human book." When necessary, we must without hesitation give a bold and thoughtful rationale for our conviction about the Scriptures. For Southern Baptists, that conviction is clearly stated in our 1963 confession of faith called *The Baptist Faith and Message*:

> The Holy Bible was written by men divinely inspired and is the record of God's revelation of Himself to man. It is a perfect treasure of divine instruction. It has God for its author, salvation for its end, and truth, without any mixture of error, for its matter. It reveals the principles by which God judges us; and therefore is, and will remain to the end of the world, the true center of Christian union, and the supreme standard by which all human conduct, creeds, and religious

opinions should be tried. The criterion by which the Bible is to be interpreted is Jesus Christ.[1]

That statement is worthy of our support, but our attention should normally be on putting the Bible's message into practice and obeying it, not defending it; teaching and preaching its truths, not arguing over the best word to use to describe its truthfulness.

Advice from 2 Timothy

Paul addressed some of these issues about the Bible in his second letter to Timothy. In his letter, He gave his young colleague in ministry some advice about how to handle the word of God properly, how to handle disagreements properly, and how to handle his own attitude properly. His advice is still timely. Let's not forget that these verses are a part of the authoritative, inspired word of God!

How to Handle the Word of God Properly

> You then, my son, be strong in the grace that is in Christ Jesus and what you have heard from me before many witnesses entrust to faithful men who will be able to teach others also . . . . Do your best to present yourself to God as one approved, a workman who has no need to be ashamed, rightly handling the word of truth. (2 Tim 2:1-2, 15)

In verse 15, "rightly handling" translates one Greek word: *orthotomeo.* It literally means "to cut straight." An *ortho*dontist straightens teeth, and an *ortho*pedist straightens bones, so *ortho*tomeo is to teach the word of God straight.

(One of our daughters wore braces from an orthodontist to straighten her teeth, and the other one wore a brace from an orthopedist to straighten her spinal scoliosis, and when we got the medical bills we could have used an *ortho*-economist to straighten our budget!)

So Paul said, we should teach the word of God straight—without distortion, without obscurity, and without modification. We are to let the Bible clear a straight path of truth without our interference.

Clement and Eusebius linked the word *orthotomeo* with the word "orthodoxy," which means "straight thinking." Straight teaching is based upon straight thinking about the Bible. To handle the word of God any other way is to be what Paul calls a workman who *needs* to be ashamed. We should be ashamed if we neglect the word or treat it casually. Ashamed if we seek comfort in its passages but ignore its challenges. Ashamed if we twist its meaning to try to make it say what we want to hear. Ashamed if we emphasize one theme of the Scripture while neglecting other themes. Ashamed if we believe hearing it is the same as obeying it.

Some of us emphasize the Bible's message of contemporary ethics but neglect its eschatological message that Jesus is coming again. *That's not straight teaching.* Others focus on their favorite millennial position about end times but neglect what the Bible says about race relations. *That's not straight teaching.* Some of us like to proclaim the humanity of Jesus and His great moral teachings but neglect the Bible's supernatural message of atonement. *That's not straight teaching.* Others emphasize the evangelistic responsibilities set out in the Bible but neglect the social responsibilities. *That's not straight teaching.* Jesus called us to teach *all* the things He commanded, and an unbalanced message is not *orthotomeo*. It's not rightly handling the word of God, and we need to be ashamed.

Paul named two of these shameful teachers in verses 17-18: Hymenaeus and Philetus. We don't know much about them, but apparently they didn't believe in the resurrection of the dead, so they conveniently "demythologized" those Scriptures and taught that the resurrection was merely an allegory typifying the soul rising from the darkness of ignorance to the light of knowledge. They bent the message to fit their own presuppositions. And according to Paul, such teaching is not straight. It's crooked—swerving from the truth and distorting the faith of their hearers. Such workmen *need* to be ashamed because they improperly handle the word of God.

How to Handle Disagreements Properly

Paul let Timothy know that not everybody would agree with him. He would encounter opposition like a soldier on the battlefield. "No soldier on service gets entangled in civilian pursuits" (v. 3). He would meet competition like an athlete on the playing field. "An athlete is not crowned unless he competes according to the rules" (v. 5). He would encounter stubborn resistance like a farmer plowing a rocky field. "It is the hard-working farmer who ought to have the first share of the crops" (v. 6).

In the church, Paul pointed out, there would be "vessels of gold and silver but also of wood and earthenware, and some for noble use, some for ignoble" (v. 20). That is, he would encounter people who agreed with him and people who disagreed. Timothy would need to learn how to handle this inevitable opposition. He needed to know how to disagree agreeably if he were to be a teacher who rightly divided the word of truth.

And if Timothy needed to learn that in the first century, we twenty-first-century Baptists, who have made ugly disagreement an art form, need to learn it even more. We've forgotten how to handle our differences in a civil, gracious, kind manner. Our self-righteous pride, demagoguery, haranguing, and unjust criticism have given us a shameful reputation before the world.

We have too many factions checking out the orthodoxy of other groups. There are too many pastors lurking in the shadows like ecclesiastical traffic cops trying to catch their fellow pastor in some error so they can hand out a ticket for supposed heresy. We have too many self-appointed judges too quick to brand some other believer with a degrading label.

Here is Paul's advice to Timothy and to us:

(1) *Don't be defensive.* When opposition arises or disagreements develop, don't jump to the defense of orthodoxy. The word of God will stand without your apologetic defense. "God's firm foundation stands" (v.19). "The Word of God is not fettered (bound)" (v. 9). It doesn't need to be defended so much as it needs to be studied, learned, heard, proclaimed, incarnated, and obeyed! As Charles Haddon Spurgeon once said, "There is no need to defend a lion when he's being attacked. All you need to do is to open the gate and let him out."

Even the heresy of Hymenaeus and Philetus will not overthrow the truth of Scripture. Heresies are often not as dangerous as are sensitive, insecure defenders who use the Bible primarily as a source for proof texts to win a debate. Prideful people with little humility who are constantly defending their position instead of pleading for loyalty to Christ are actually hindering the cause of Christ. Don't be defensive. Stand faithfully proclaiming and teaching the truth, and the truth will be its own best defense. "Just open the gate and let it out!"

(2) *Don't be argumentative or contentious.*

> Have nothing to do with stupid, senseless controversies; you know that they breed quarrels, and the Lord's servant must not be quarrelsome but kindly to every one, an apt teacher, forbearing, correcting his opponents with gentleness. (2 Tim 2:23-24)

We twenty-first-century Christians need to stop walking about with theological chips on our shoulders. We should practice Christian civility, be kind and magnanimous, disagree agreeably. With mutual respect for the opposition, we should approach those with whom we disagree with good faith, courtesy, and humility. That's part of what it means to respect the priesthood of each believer, which allows every person the right to speak the truth as the Holy Spirit guides them.

(3) *Don't fight over words.* "Avoid disputing about words, which does no good, but only ruins the hearers" (2 Tim 2:14-17). Paul warned that it was not the error of Hymenaeus and Philetus that would destroy the church but the petty hair-splitting disputes about unanswerable questions. He called this *logomachein,* literally "striving with words" or "sword-fighting over words." Such disputes are senseless, stupid, unedifying, godless chatter. It's nothing more than profane jargon, and it undermines the faith! How pleased Satan is when the army of God starts fighting among themselves over semantics. Such conflict over words destroys the health of the church. It doesn't feed the souls of the hearers; it feeds *on* their souls—eating away like a cancer the health of the church. (vv. 16-17)

The way to handle disagreements is in verses 24-26. Better than argument is kindness that attracts rather than repels, that calms rather than irritates. Better than impatient, harsh intolerance that lashes out with sarcasm are forbearance and gentleness. For only with these qualities will God be able to work through us to lead others to repentance and to the knowledge of the truth. Learn how to handle disagreements properly.

How to Handle Our Own Attitude Properly

When we teach about Jesus, the techniques of teaching are not nearly so important as the spirit and attitude of the teacher. That may not be as important when one is teaching chemistry or algebra or engineering, but when we teach about Jesus, the spirit and the attitude of the teacher are absolutely crucial. Nobody wants to learn good grooming from someone who looks like they've been in a seven-day hatchet fight and lost their hatchet on the first day! Nobody wants to learn body-building from a flabby, sedentary weakling who's unable to do one pushup. Somebody said, never go to a doctor in whose waiting room all the plants are dead.

Neither do people want to learn about Jesus from a mean-spirited self-righteous critic. To be an effective teacher of the word, we must have more than a Master of Arts degree; we must master the arts of Christian civility: humility, gentleness, patience, and love. The Bible makes it clear that you and I have a stewardship of attitude that we must fulfill if we teach the word of God straight. Look at the astounding list of qualities this passage indicates are required of a disciple-teacher who rightly divides the word of truth:

1. Sacrificial devotion, singular loyalty like a victorious soldier (v. 4)
2. Selfless discipline like a winning athlete (v. 5)
3. Striving diligence like a hard-working farmer (v. 6)
4. Purified, consecrated, useful (v. 21)
5. Righteous, faithful, loving, peaceful, pure (v. 22)
6. Kind, patient, apt, gentle (vv. 24-25)
7. Depending on God's grace (v. 1)
8. Reflecting Jesus Christ as example (v. 8)

We must obey the Bible, not just defend it.

Advice from Joshua

Another place where the Bible speaks about the importance of obeying its message is in Joshua 1:7-8:

> Only be strong and very courageous, being careful to do according to all the law which Moses my servant commanded you; turn not from it to the right hand or to the left, that you may have good success wherever you go. This book of the law shall not depart out of your mouth, but you shall meditate on it day and night, that you may be careful to do according to all that is written in it; for then you shall make your way prosperous, and then you shall have good success.

God commanded Joshua to *memorize* the words: "This book of the law shall not depart out of your mouth." The picture is that of Joshua repeating the words again and again until they were not only on his lips but hidden in his heart. Second, Joshua was to *meditate* on the message of the Scriptures: "You shall meditate on it day and night." Meditation involves prayerful, spirit-led study of Scripture, not just to get theoretical knowledge or ammunition for a debate, but so that God may speak through the verses to guide and direct you in decisions. Third, Joshua was to *mind* the Bible, obey its commands: "be careful to do according to all that is written in it. . . . turn not from it to the right hand or to the left."

Notice that God didn't command Joshua to defend the authenticity of the Law or to debate its authority. He commanded him only to memorize it, to meditate on it, and to mind it. After all, Scripture, in all its power and grandeur—then as now—needs no defense or protection. Instead, it needs to be studied, learned, heard, proclaimed, incarnated, and—most of all—obeyed! That's the higher ground on which believers ought to plant their feet.

Biblical Authority in Perspective

One characteristic of twenty-first-century society is its loss of absolutes. Scandals in business, in politics, and even in the church suggest that many assume there is no ultimate accountability, no authority that determines right and wrong. Is there a person or a document that has authority to prescribe religious belief and action? What is the final court of appeal when it comes to standards of belief and practice?

While some would point to the church, a creed, experience, or reason as final authority, most believers would say, "The final authority is God," "Jesus Christ is my authority," "I'm guided by the Holy Spirit," or "The Bible is my authority." Which is the right answer? How can we best express our view of ultimate authority?

Bernard Ramm, former professor at Baylor University, offered a helpful idea called a "Pattern of Authority." It's certainly true that God is our ultimate authority, that Jesus, the living, personal revelation of God who sums up the Old Testament, is our authority, and that the New Testament where the apostles expressed their inspired witness is our authority. It's also true that the Holy Spirit illumines the believer to hear God speak through Scripture. He is our authority. So Ramm suggested that our view of ultimate authority should include all the above in a "Pattern": Our authority is the sovereign, triune God, revealed in Jesus Christ, communicated through His inspired word, and confirmed by the Holy Spirit in Christian experience.

So the Bible is our authority, but not in isolation. We must understand its proper relationship to the Father, the Holy Spirit, and the Lord Jesus. The Bible cannot take the place of Jesus Christ. We're not saved by believing the Scriptures, but by believing in Jesus. As *The Baptist Faith and Message* says, "The criterion by which the Bible is to be interpreted is Jesus Christ."

It's possible for our legitimate desire to defend the Bible to become misguided and wrong. Don't forget: no matter how legitimate our goals may be, they can never justify illegitimate methods for accomplishing those goals. The end never justifies the means. In our enthusiasm to protect the Bible, we may be ignoring the very message

God intended it to convey. I will never forget a criticism from a secular newspaper writer who was reporting on the squabbling at one of our Baptist Conventions. He had interviewed an outspoken luminary in the takeover party, and his conclusion was a stinging rebuke: "That man obviously knows the Bible by heart, but his heart doesn't know the Bible!"

If we use the Bible as a legalistic weapon for enforcing our view of orthodoxy, we tend to violate the principles Jesus stood for and taught. Again and again, He condemned the legalistic, theological hairsplitting of the scribes and Pharisees. They obviously loved and respected the Scriptures, and that's good. They worked hard at protecting and promoting biblical authority, and that's all right. But they took the simple law of God, and through their own interpretation, they complicated and distorted it with minute and unreasonable demands. They were more interested in defending the Bible than obeying it, and that's bad.

Jesus vigorously denounced these would-be watchdogs of orthodoxy who strained at gnats and made the law a tedious burden on those they were supposed to be helping. They were too quick to cast out specks from other people's eyes when they had huge splinters in their own eyes. He rebuked them because they had no right as fallible men to interpret what God had said and make that interpretation infallibly binding on someone else. Their goal may have been noble, but their methods became sinful. These same principles apply today. We need to be more vigorous in obeying the Bible than we sometimes are in defending it.

In summer 1980, in Canton, China, my wife and I had the privilege of worshiping with 2,000 Chinese Christians in the Tung Shan Church. It had been closed for years, and now, under a new government policy, it had been given permission to reopen. There were no Bibles in the congregation. I noted, however, that as the Baptist pastor, Matthew Tong, preached an evangelistic sermon, the people gave close attention to the printed programs they had been handed when they came in. A Chinese friend informed us that each Sunday the pastor printed on the program a lengthy passage of Scripture in Cantonese as his text for that day. The worshipers were eagerly collecting these weekly bulletins Sunday by Sunday as the only Bible they had.

I watched as these fellow believers who had long been deprived of the Bible carefully protected, tucked away, and carried home their limited but valuable copy of God's word. Somehow all the discussions about what terms to use to describe the Bible's authority seemed irrelevant. All of the criticism and judgmental condemnation among Christian brothers and sisters who do not agree seemed out of place. That worship service led me to a renewed commitment to God's word. It called me to dedicate myself again in humility, appreciation, reliance, and submission to the study, understanding, practice, and proclamation of God's holy word. I remembered again a prayer printed in a Bible that belonged to my father:

> Blessed Lord who has caused all Holy Scriptures to be written for our learning, grant that we may in such wise hear them, read, mark, learn, and inwardly digest them so that by the patience and comfort of thy Holy Word we may embrace and ever hold fast the blessed hope of everlasting life which thou hast given us in our Savior Jesus Christ, in whose name we pray. Amen.[2]

The higher ground of Christian civility involves obeying the Bible, not just defending it.

Notes

[1] Herschel Hobbs, *The Baptist Faith and Message* (Nashville: Convention Press, 1963) 18.

[2] Thomas Cranmer, *The Book of Common Prayer* (New York: James Pott & Co., 1892) 92.

Fruit of the Spirit, Not Worldly Standards

In these harsh, self-centered days at the beginning of the twenty-first century, virtues such as kindness seem to have vanished from the public arena. One example of this lack of kindness pops up occasionally on the Internet where anonymous communication provides immunity to "surfers." A surprising number take the opportunity in an email to "flame" others with virulent language they probably wouldn't use if face to face with their antagonist. As a result, simple kindness has been deleted from millions of computer screens across the Internet.

But the absence of kindness is not limited to the impersonal cyber-realm of polyworld. Listen to candidates who trash their opponents in current political debates. Or, ironically, tune in to speeches by Christian luminaries in some of our recent denominational controversies.

Isn't it ironic that the "hardliners" who imposed the destructive dispute on the Southern Baptist family by loudly promoting the Bible's truthfulness often paid so little attention to the truth the Bible teaches? God's word plainly demands that followers of the Lord Jesus Christ exhibit certain Christlike qualities, most of which are identified as "the fruit of the Spirit." But even simple kindness, the most basic of these qualities, was glaringly absent.

The Fruit of the Spirit

The fruit of the Spirit is love (*agape*), joy (*chara*), peace (*eirene*), patience (*makrothumia*), kindness (*chrestotes*), goodness (*agathosune*), faithfulness (*pistis*), gentleness (*prautes*), self-control (*egkrateia*) (Gal 5:22).

It's interesting to notice that the term "fruit" is singular in form. It's not "fruits" of the Spirit, although we generally list them as though they were separate, free-standing qualities. The verse in Galatians actually refers to these qualities as one combined fruit or "harvest" of the Spirit. The singular form stresses the fact that the fruit is one cluster, constituting an organic whole that springs from one root. While it has many individual parts like a diamond has many facets, it is, in fact, one cumulative harvest.

So the idea is that when the Holy Spirit takes up residence in a believer's life at conversion, the evidence of His presence in that life is a beautiful harvest—the harvest or fruit of the Spirit. In other words, the fruit is the sign that the Holy Spirit is developing in the believer the likeness of the Lord Jesus Christ. The writer of Hebrews called it "the peaceful fruit of righteousness" (Heb 12:11).

So it's not a matter of a Christian picking and choosing which of these virtues he or she will exhibit in daily living. *All* of these virtues that make up the harvest of the Spirit should grace the life of the believer. Sometimes we romanticize spirituality, imagining it to be an ethereal, "otherworldly" quality that is beyond the reach of ordinary Christians. But the Bible plants true spirituality in the common soil of everyday living, and the harvest that springs from that soil is made up of these common virtues. They are the material from which spirituality is forged and they are, at the same time, the evidences of true holiness.

In his sage advice to his young protégé, Timothy, Paul reminded him that a good disciple is marked by godly conduct. He wrote,

> Be a good servant of Christ Jesus . . . . Train yourself in godliness;
> for while bodily training is of some value, godliness is of value in
> every way, as it holds promise for the present life and also for the life

to come . . . . Let no one despise your youth, but set the believers an example in speech and conduct, in love, in faith, and in purity. (1 Tim 4:6, 7-8, 12)

That advice addressed a problem Timothy was struggling with—authenticating his ministry. "Let no one despise your youth" (v. 12). Apparently some were questioning his legitimacy as a leader in the church because he was young—maybe in his early twenties. He was having trouble getting respect among the churches. They wanted their leaders to be older.

There is an English translation of an ancient manual of church order from the fourth century called *The Apostolic Canons.* It advises the early churches that a man ought not become a bishop until he is over "50 years of age, for such a one," the manual explains, will be "past youthful disorders!" They wanted their leaders older.[1]

Timothy was young, so how could he gain respect? How could he validate his discipleship? It would not be by verbal defense, by argument, or by political spin doctors putting a positive slant on his press releases. Paul told him to silence criticism by conduct, by godly living. "Be a good disciple [minister] of Christ Jesus" (v. 6).

How good does a genuine disciple of Jesus have to be in order to validate that discipleship? What is the measure of true spirituality? First, Paul advised Timothy to set the believers an example in conduct and speech in three areas: (1) love—*agape*—unconquerable benevolence toward others, (2) faith—*pistis*—uncompromising fidelity to Jesus, and (3) purity—*hagnia*—unquestioning imitation of the morality of Jesus.

How good do we have to be? Second, Paul said a believer should be godly. "Train yourself [literally exercise yourself] in godliness" (v. 7). We should be like God. Not in God's exalted essence, not in omnipotence and omniscience, but as God is holy, we should be holy. As God is righteous, just, and merciful, so we should be righteous, just, and merciful. We're to be like God. "Be perfect as your heavenly Father is perfect" (Matt 5:48).

How good do we have to be? The Bible also says we should be Christlike. We're to be like Jesus. Not in His sinless perfection, not in

His supernatural deity or His miraculous power—but we're to imitate the way He obeyed the Father, the way He forgave others, and the way He loved and served.

How good do we have to be? The Bible says we should be filled with the Spirit; we should demonstrate the fruit of the Spirit. The natural outgrowth of your spiritual life is the harvest of love, joy, peace, patience, kindness, goodness, faithfulness, gentleness, and self-control.

Let's examine those nine elements that make up the "peaceful fruit of righteousness." According to some interpreters, the list seems to be given in a triplicate form. It's made up of three groups of three graces each:

(1) The first group describes the Christian life in its personal relationship to God: love, joy, and peace.

(2) The second group describes the Christian life in its relationship to others: patience, kindness, goodness.

(3) The third group describes the Christian life in its relationship to difficulties faced: faithfulness, gentleness, self-control.

While this grouping may seem a bit arbitrary, and it tends to overlook the fact that "fruit" is a single union of the various elements, it's still helpful to examine them in this triplicate arrangement.

Love (agape), Joy (chara), and Peace (eirene)

This group describes the Christian life in its personal relationship to God.

Love (*agape*). The Greek language in which the New Testament was written is called *koine* Greek. It was the everyday "street language" of the ordinary population. Since the New Testament was conveyed in this common linguistic form, it was therefore more readily understood by first-century readers than the high-tone classical Greek of philosophers and scholars. Furthermore, because of its grammatical distinctions, varied vocabulary, linguistic nuances, and universal use in the Mediterranean world, *koine* Greek was a perfect vehicle for conveying the gospel to every echelon of humanity in the first-century world.

An example of its varied vocabulary is the multiple options it offered for our English word "love." Each of these Greek words had a different shade of meaning. There was *eros,* the word for physical, sexual love, and *storge,* the filial word for the love family members shared for each other. Neither of these appears in the New Testament. Two Greek words for love do appear in the New Testament, *philia* and *agape.* The first is a general word for the warm feeling of affection one feels for a friend or a respected acquaintance. It's been called "platonic" love, and it's often translated "friendship" in the English Scriptures. We find it in the name of the Pennsylvania city Philadelphia the city of brotherly love.

The second word, *agape,* doesn't really have an English equivalent. It describes the highest form of self-giving, unconditional love that's not so much an emotion as it is an attitude of sacrificial concern for another person's welfare. The New Testament identifies this word *agape* as the superlative theme of the Christian faith. It's radical, "good Samaritan" love that's based on an intentionally chosen attitude or world view of open, unselfish concern for others. *Agape* love naturally expresses itself in actions to help others. For example, "God so loved (*agape*) the world that He gave . . . ."

There's a fascinating interplay between these two words *philia* and *agape* in John 21:15-17 when the risen Lord questions Simon Peter. Two times Jesus used the word *agape* to ask, "Do you love me?" (Meaning with that highest form of self-giving, unconditional commitment.) Two times Peter used the word *philia* to answer, "You know I love you." (That is, I have a friendly affection for you.) Peter was unwilling to claim an unconditional, self-giving love for Jesus, and he chose instead to use the lesser word for friendship. The third time Jesus asked, "Do you love me?" He came down to Peter's level and used the word *philia.* Peter was grieved by that concession, but in his third answer, he still refused to use *agape* and instead chose *philia*: "I have a friendly affection for you."

John Stott, the British theologian, asked the question, "What is the authenticating mark of a true believer?" What is the chief distinguishing characteristic of a Christian, the hallmark that lets a person know you're a genuine believer? Stott answered the question by referring to Paul's hymn of love in 1 Corinthians 13.

Some would say it's truth, orthodoxy, correct belief, and to an extent that's right. It's important to believe the Bible and understand the truth of God's word. But in that famous chapter on *agape* love in 1 Corinthians 13:2, Paul wrote, "If I understand all mysteries and all knowledge but have not love (*agape*), I am nothing." Love is greater than knowledge and truth.

Others claim the mark of a true believer is faith. Certainly most would agree with the reformation principle *sola fide*—faith alone. We can have a personal relationship with God only through faith in Jesus Christ, not by good works. Faith is crucial, but Paul wrote, "If I have all faith, so as to remove mountains, but have not love, I am nothing." Love is greater than faith.

Is the mark of a true believer personal experience? Yes, to an extent. Each individual must have an individual encounter with God. You can't depend on the experience of your parents, your friends, or your fellow church members. You have to experience the Lord for yourself. Some people say that a genuine spiritual experience should involve glossolalia, speaking in tongues and other "charismatic gifts." But Paul wrote, "If I speak in the tongues of men and of angels . . . if I have prophetic powers, but have not love, I am a noisy gong or a clanging cymbal." Love is greater than the experience.

What about good works? Isn't the mark of a true believer the good deeds a person renders? After all, didn't James say, "Faith without works is dead"? Don't the Scriptures say, "By their fruit you will know them"? Yes, true, but notice Paul warned in verse 3, "If I give away all I have, and if I deliver my body to be burned, but have not love, I gain nothing." Love is greater than works.

Love holds a supreme place in the Bible. Paul advised, "And above all these, put on love (*agape*) which binds everything together in perfect harmony" (Col 3:14), and Jesus labeled it the greater of the two greatest commandments: "You shall love (*agape*) the Lord your God with all your heart, and with all your soul, and with all your mind…you shall love (*agape*) neighbor as yourself" (Matt 22:37-39). So based on the list above, the fruit of the Spirit begins with this "queen of the Christian graces," love (*agape*), a grace so supernatural that it can exist only through a personal relationship with the God who *is* love. That's why Henry Drummond called love "the greatest thing in the world."[2]

Joy (*chara*), or gladness, is a word found often in the New Testament, especially on the lips of Jesus who frequently commanded, "Rejoice and be glad." Paul echoed these words of Jesus with an emphatic "double take": "Rejoice in the Lord always, and again I will say rejoice!" (Phil 4:4). The dictionary definition of our English word joy is "a very glad feeling; happiness, great pleasure; delight," but the biblical idea is far different from this worldly brand of pleasure or happiness. Earthly joy can be so fragmentary and fleeting that sometimes it's difficult to distinguish it from sorrow!

Citing humorist Mark Twain as an example, Pastor Earl Davis pointed out that a person can be a great humorist making others laugh and yet be joyless, cynical, and bitter. He quoted the jovial Mark Twain's surprising sad worldview:

> The burden of pain, care, misery, grows heavier year by year; at length ambition is dead; pride is dead; vanity is dead; longing for release is in their place. (Death) comes at last—the only unpoisoned gift earth ever had for them—and they vanish from a world where they were of no consequence, where they achieved nothing, where they were a mistake and a failure and a foolishness: where they left no sign that they ever existed—a world which will lament them a day and forget them forever.[3]

By contrast, Christian joy is a deep sense of fulfillment and satisfaction that creates a feeling of contented happiness. This joy is poured into our lives when Jesus comes to live within us. Jesus promised to impart His joy to us, that it would be full, and that it would remain. It's permanent and fills every corner of our lives. It can thrive in the midst of suffering and sorrow. According to the Bible, Christians can be "exceeding glad" even when they're being persecuted (Matt 6:12, Acts 5:41, 1 Thess 1:6).

Peace (*eirene*). This Greek word can mean (1) national tranquility, freedom from war, (2) harmony or concord between individuals, (3) tranquility or prosperity expressed in the Hebrew term *shalom,* (4) eschatological peace that will be enjoyed in heaven, (5) the state of the dead who die in Christ, and (6) the tranquil state of a person who is assured of salvation through Christ and who is therefore afraid of nothing and is content with life. It seems this last definition is the one that appears here. True peace comes not from the absence of trouble, but from the presence of God, and since it's supernatural, it passes all understanding (Phil 4:7).

Patience (makrothumia), Kindness (chrestotes), and Goodness (agathosune)

This second group describes the Christian life in its relationship to others.

Patience (*makrothumia*) is the first in this triad. The Greek word literally means "to remain under" and describes the trait of long-suffering endurance toward people and circumstances that bring us grief. According to Paul, the believer is not easily provoked, is not irritable or resentful, and bears and endures all things (1 Cor 13).

It seems so out of character for Christian brothers and sisters to claim they've been left out of church positions or denominational posts and, insisting "it's our turn now," to push others out and maneuver themselves into places of honor or leadership. Even if they were treated unfairly, the fruit of the Spirit is not likely to be born in the life of those who grasp for positions, repaying evil for evil or scorn for scorn. Proverbs 26:4 says, "Answer not a fool according to his folly, lest you be like him yourself."

Kindness (*chrestotes*) is defined as being sympathetic, friendly, gentle, generous, cordial, and tenderhearted. It's the very word used when Jesus said, "My yoke is *easy*" (Matt 11:30). Goodness by itself can be stern, but *chrestotes* bathes goodness in kindness. This is the type of goodness that Jesus used toward the sinning woman who anointed His feet (Luke 7:37–50). No doubt Simon the Pharisee was a good man, but Jesus was more than good. He exhibited *chrestotes*.

The adjective "kind" is *chrestos* in Greek. It was a popular name for slaves in biblical times, and it has led some interpreters to suggest that this entire list of virtues that make up the fruit of the Spirit is a list of "slave virtues." Alan Cole goes even further to suggest that there may have been a popular pun in the first century comparing the popular slave name *Chrestos* with the servant Messiah named *Christos*.[4] Could it be that the "smart alecs" in Antioch who first named the followers of Jesus used this pun on the word for "slaves" and the word for followers of Jesus the Christ?

One of the clearest verses in Scripture is the command, "Be kind to another, tender-hearted, forgiving one another" (Eph 4:32). The Bible indicates that even Almighty God, the Creator, is kind! Can you imagine that? God is kind! "Thy loving kindness extends to the heavens . . ." (Ps. 36:7). "I am the Lord who practices loving kindness . . ." (Jer 9:24).

But sadly, this simple Christian grace is sometimes missing among those who loudly boast about their belief in the authority of Scripture. They claim the Bible should be obeyed, but then they act with such unkindness. These authoritarian legalists make up only a fraction of Christian leaders, but they're often in the media spotlight, giving authentic ministry a bad name. No wonder a recent survey from the Princeton Center for Religion Research shows that only half the population now ranks clergy "high" or "very high" in ethics. That's a drop from two-thirds in 1985.

The city of Dallas, Texas, recently launched a campaign to rediscover kindness as a regular and crucial quality of life in the city. Dallas called on her citizens to "commit wanton acts of kindness" as one solution to the troubled relationships that often threaten community life. Surely Bible-believing followers of the Lord Jesus Christ should do no less.

Goodness *(agathosune)* is closely akin to kindness. In a way, kindness describes the inward disposition, and goodness describes the actions that demonstrate that inward disposition. A number of interpreters point out a distinction between being righteous and being good. Paul may have had this in mind when he wrote, "One would hardly die for a *righteous* man—though perhaps for a *good* man one will dare even to die." (Rom 5:7) There's a Pharisaical kind of righteousness that keeps all the rules, but is stern and condemning. Goodness, adds to righteousness a personal touch of warmth and generosity toward others. It carries the additional meaning of "benevolent" and "generous." In fact Plato likened this word to *agastos*, which means "likeable" or "admirable."[5]

These three facets of the fruit of the Spirit call for a relationship with others that is long-suffering, tender-hearted, and good-hearted with a spirit of admirable generosity.

Faithfulness (pistis), Gentleness (prautes), Self-control (egkrateia)

The third group describes the Christian life in its relationship to difficulties faced.

Faithfulness (*pistis*). Here *pistis* is not faith in the theological sense, but faithfulness or trustworthiness. It's the quality of dependability in discharging the duties of discipleship and church life. Paul may have been enlarging on this virtue when he said, "Be steadfast, immovable, always abounding in the work of the Lord, knowing that in the Lord your labor is not in vain" (1 Cor 15:58), and "Let us not grow weary in doing good, for in due time we shall reap if we do not lose heart" (Gal 6:9).

Too often our heroes are the Christian leaders who make headlines, the mega stars who have the chief places, who appear on *Larry King Live*. We idolize Christian celebrities with lifestyles of the rich and famous because we consider them "successful." (Paul sarcastically refers to them as "super apostles" in 2 Corinthians 11:5.)

But we forget that the Bible says successful Christians are those who are genuinely faithful. God spells success f-a-i-t-h-f-u-l. He doesn't demand that we be smart, although He honors intelligence and education. He doesn't demand that we be talented, although He rejoices in our gifts. He doesn't demand that we be successful, although He wants us to achieve and not fail. But what God does demand is faithfulness. "Be faithful unto death, and I will give you the crown of life" (Rev 2:10).

It was not the trumpeting Pharisee with his self-directed public relations campaign that Jesus praised, but the nameless widow, the one who quietly, without headlines, faithfully donated her pennies to the Lord.

I've always been encouraged by that Scripture passage in John 10:40-42 that tells how Jesus returned to the area where John the Baptist had ministered. It was long after John's death, but the people still remembered him with great appreciation. They said of John the Baptist, "John never worked a miracle, but everything he told us about Jesus was true." His success was not found in fanfare, but in faithfulness.

Toward the end of his life, the Apostle Paul himself acknowledged that he had fought a good fight and kept the faith and finished the race. Notice he didn't say he'd won the race—only that he'd finished it. He didn't quit. I found an interesting verse in Psalm 57:7: "My heart is faithful, O God, My heart is faithful. Therefore I will sing and make melody!" Maybe it's no stretch of interpretation to suggest that the verse is saying faithfulness is like music in the ears of God.

Gentleness (*prautes*). The various English versions of the New Testament offer different translations of this word *prautes*: "meekness," "humility," "modesty," but most translate it "gentleness." Twice the word is used of Jesus Himself (Matt 11:29; 21:5). When it appears in the writings of the classical Greek philosophers, it always has a lovely quality to it. For example, the word is used to describe "gentle" breezes or "gentle" voices or "mild" and "gracious" people. William Barclay claims that in classical Greek the word *prautes* "has a caress in it," pointing out that Xenophon used the word in the sense of a tender embrace.[6] In his typical way of finding meaning between extremes, Aristotle said *prautes* was midway between excessive anger on the one hand and excessive angerlessness on the other! In other words, a person who is *praus* or gentle is always angry at the right time and never angry at the wrong time.

My Greek professor in seminary reminded us that the word *prautes* was used to describe a horse that had been tamed. In the West, when a wild stallion was lassoed and brought into the corral, a cowboy would "break" it by putting a saddle on its back, a bit and a bridle in its mouth, and riding the bucking beast until it became obedient to the rider's commands. All the muscular strength of the horse was still intact, but it was now tamed and under control. So according to the New Testament, a gentle or meek person is not a timid, spineless weakling, but a courageous person with strength of steel whose power is channeled and under control. Just as a tamed horse obeys the commands of the rider, so a "gentle" believer obeys the commands of God, so that all that vigorous strength is focused on God's will.

Self-control (*egkrateia*). The King James Version translates *egkrateia* "temperance," an old-fashioned English word that historically described sobriety or abstinence from the use of alcohol. In a broader application, "self-control" is an important spiritual quality that helps a believer grapple with all kinds of natural passions and temptations—especially the grosser "works of the flesh" Paul listed in Galatians 5:19-21: fornication, impurity, licentiousness, drunkenness, and carousing. "Those who habitually live like this [Greek present tense indicates continuous action] will not inherit the kingdom of God" (v. 21). But "those who belong to Christ Jesus have crucified the flesh with its passions and desires," and they will habitually bear the fruit of the Spirit, which includes self-control (v. 24).

Conclusion

One antidote to the poison of rancorous incivility in our country and in our churches and denominations is a rebirth of a thoroughgoing Christian civility. Nowhere is that kind of civility presented more succinctly than in this concept of the fruit of the Spirit. If followers of the Lord Jesus Christ would exhibit these nine facets of spiritual fruit in the national arena and in our ecclesial debates, it would not be long before the rude grandstanding and finger-pointing would give way to a kinder, gentler environment.

One year, my wife, Betty, and I took an autumn foliage trip to New England. One of our stops was Freeport, Maine, among other things noted as a shopper's paradise. The famous sporting goods store, L.L. Bean, is headquartered there, and it stays open twenty-four hours every day. Surrounding that primary retail establishment are outlet malls and specialty shops of every kind.

One of my favorites was a small location that specialized in hand-carved water fowl, beautiful reproductions of ducks and geese. I'd always wanted a mallard decoy for my office, but the prices were extravagantly expensive. However, I noticed a sign on the back wall of the shop with big red letters: "SECONDS—HALF PRICE!" Sure enough, I found a small reproduction of a green-headed duck that was budget-priced, and upon close examination, it revealed no obvious flaws.

I bought it and then ambled to a table in the middle of the store where a group of woodcarvers were at work chipping and painting their beautiful works of art. Thinking one of them might have fashioned my mallard, I engaged them in small talk. "What are you carving today?" Expecting to hear them respond with names like Wood Duck, Mallard, or Pin-tail, I was surprised when they looked sheepishly at each other and answered, "Well, frankly, today we're carving seconds. They're selling so well, we're just making seconds!"

I'd never heard of that marketing strategy—intentionally making flawed merchandise to sell at half-price on the "seconds" table. I went away thinking that it might be a clever technique in the world of commerce, but not in Christian discipleship. No true believer wants intentionally to be second best—flawed. We want to bear a likeness to Jesus; we want to bear the fruit of the Spirit. We want to be good disciples of Jesus so that when we meet the Lord, He will say, "Well done"—not flawed, not mediocre—but "well done, good, faithful servant."

The motto of the church organization for boys called "Royal Ambassadors" comes from Tennyson's *Idylls of the King*: "Live pure, speak truth, right wrong, follow the King—else wherefore born?"

Notes

[1] Alexander Roberts, ed., *The Ante-Nicene Fathers* (Grand Rapids: Wm. B. Eerdmans, 1886); *The Constitution of the Holy Apostles*, sec. 1, "On Examining Candidates for the Episcopal Office: That a Bishop Must Be Instructed and Experienced in the Word," <http://www.ccel.org/ccel/schaff/anf07.ix.iii.i.html>.

[2] Henry Drummond, *The Greatest Thing in the World* (Gainesville: Bridge-Logos Publishers, 2005) i.

[3] Earl C. Davis, *Layman's Library of Christian Doctrine: Live in the Spirit* (Nashville: Broadman, 1986) 102.

[4] R. Alan Cole, *The Letter of Paul to the Galatians* (Leicester: Inter-Varsity Press, 1989) 220.

[5] Joseph Henry Thayer, *A Greek-English Lexicon of the New Testament* (New York: American Book Co., 1889) 2.

[6] William Barclay, *A New Testament Wordbook* (New York: Harper & Brothers, n.d.) 103.

Spiritual Weapons, Not Worldly Weapons

A significant portion of the incivility encountered in religious dialogue today can be traced to a growing trend among some Christian activists to utilize secular, worldly methods in their Christian work. Their motives seem commendable. They want to obey the command of Jesus to go into the world and make disciples, to preach the gospel, and to start New Testament churches. They want to defend and pass on to future generations "the faith which was once for all delivered to the saints" (Jude 1:3). Who could argue with these commendable goals? The problem, however, is not with motives but with methods.

Too many of these activists have chosen to accomplish their goals by employing carnal weapons in spite of clear biblical prohibitions against it. Jesus rebuked Simon Peter for resorting to worldly, military solutions. He said, "Put your sword back into its place, for all who take the sword will perish by the sword" (Matt 26: 52).

Paul cautioned believers who "act in worldly fashion." He warned, "For though we live in the world, we are not carrying on a worldly war. For the weapons of our warfare are not worldly but have divine power to destroy strongholds" (2 Cor 10:3-4).

Paul renounced "disgraceful, underhanded ways," and he refused "to practice cunning or to tamper with God's word, but instead he employed the open statement of the truth" (2 Cor 4:2).

In carrying out his ministry he did not depend on secular methods such as "lofty words of wisdom." He decided instead to depend on spiritual methods, "the demonstration of the Spirit and of power so that your faith might not rest in the wisdom of men, but in the power of God" (1 Cor 2:3-5).

In his letter to the Corinthian church, Paul encouraged believers to "put no obstacle in anyone's way, so that no fault may be found with our ministry, but as servants of God, commend ourselves . . . by purity, knowledge, forbearance, kindness, the Holy Spirit, genuine love, truthful speech, and the power of God; with the *weapons of righteousness* for the right hand and for the left . . ." (2 Cor 6:3-7).

Paul made it clear that quarrelsome disputes, wrangling, and a "craving for controversy" belong to the natural, fleshly realm, not the realm of the Spirit. "You are still worldly. For since there is jealousy and quarreling among you, are you not worldly? Are you not acting like mere men? This carnal behavior is even more damaging because it is done in front of unbelievers!" (1 Cor 3:3 NIV). "For I am afraid that when I come I may not find you as I want you to be . . . . I fear that there may be quarreling, jealousy, outbursts of anger, factions, slander, gossip, arrogance and disorder" (2 Cor 12:20 NIV).

He urged Timothy to renounce a person who is "puffed up with conceit, knows nothing, has a morbid craving for controversy and for disputes about words, which produce envy, dissension, slander, base suspicions, and wrangling among men" (1 Tim 6:3-5). In his second letter to Timothy, Paul challenged him

> to avoid disputing about words, which does no good, but only ruins the hearers . . . to avoid such godless chatter, for it will lead people into more and more ungodliness, and their talk will eat its way like gangrene . . . . Have nothing to do with stupid, senseless controversies; you know that they breed quarrels. And the Lord's servant must not be quarrelsome, but kindly to everyone. (2 Tim 2:14-26)

Paul instructed the Galatian believers to preserve freedom as a valuable concept, and he condemned wrangling and dissension as methods of coercion that destroyed that freedom: "But if you bite and devour one another, take heed that you are not consumed by one another" (Gal 5:15).

These New Testament passages are preceded by admonitions from the Old Testament: "Starting a quarrel is like breaching a dam; so drop the matter before a dispute breaks out" (Prov 17:14 NIV). "As charcoal to hot embers and wood to fire, so is a quarrelsome man for kindling strife" (Prov 26:21). "He who stirs up trouble in his own family will inherit only wind" (Prov 11:29). "Not by might nor by power, but by my Spirit, says the Lord of hosts" (Zech 4:6).

Any one of these verses would be reason enough to resolutely employ only spiritual weapons and to resist the temptation to use the weapons of the world. What are the spiritual weapons available to us in our Christian work? From the verses above and from other biblical passages, we can construct a partial inventory of Christian armaments:

- The open statement of the truth
- Purity, knowledge, forbearance, kindness, genuine love, truthful speech
- Weapons of righteousness for the right hand and the left
- Worship
- Prayer
- Persuasion, witness, preaching, counseling
- Teaching, learning
- The witness of moral living as an example
- Social ministries such as feeding and clothing the needy
- The Bible itself, described as the Sword of the Lord
- The Holy Spirit
- The power of God

These spiritual armaments are superior to the world's paltry arsenal. Unlike natural methods, these supernatural weapons have remarkable capacity to "demonstrate the Spirit's power" and "to destroy strongholds."

The Southern Baptist Controversy and Worldly Weapons

One of the tragedies of the denominational upheavals in the Southern Baptist Convention during the eighties and nineties was the brazen use of secular, "precinct-style" political methodologies. It all started when the fundamentalist coalition hatched a scheme to take over the

Convention by using unadulterated political strategies. Their admitted plan was to

- Organize "precincts" with loyal supporters in every geographical area of the Convention.
- Hold secret caucuses to lay out the plans.
- Announce candidates for SBC offices, particularly the president, before the Convention meetings.
- Sponsor widespread "get-out-the-vote" rallies.
- Use mass mailing and periodical advertising to pump candidates and demonize the opponents with slander, gossip, and ridicule.
- Squelch free and objective press reports.
- Secure hotel rooms and transportation for delegates who attend the Convention meetings.
- Have them stay just long enough to vote for the president.
- Circulate "how to vote" instructions for delegates who remain for business sessions.
- Orchestrate strategies from "sky boxes" overlooking the assembly and employ "floor managers" to signal party members how they should vote—similar to strategies used in the national political conventions.
- Bend the truth and the voting rules if necessary to favor your side. (The ends justify the means, don't they!)
- Adopt a pragmatic duplicity that says, "I love you, brother," while secretly promoting strategies to hurt the one you "love."
- Reward the faithful with appointments and privileges.
- Enforce party loyalty by intimidation, threat, pressure, subtle coercion, and punishment for those who don't go along.
- Name only loyalists to the boards of Convention institutions and agencies.
- Then, once in control, silence all dissent and contrary opinions.

For the first time in our remembered denominational history, these Baptist fundamentalists ignored the time-honored principle of separation of church and state, and formed coalitions with a national political party, endorsed political candidates, and opened the door for a dangerous entanglement of Baptist churches and civil government. They took advantage of the popular wave of national political conservatism that was sweeping the country and, in effect, rode that wave to achieve victory for their ultraconservative denominational agenda.

It was a clever and effective plan, but blatantly secular. By taking up the carnal strategies the Bible so clearly condemns, they opened the door for dissension, disputes, wrangling, cunning, underhanded ways, quarrels, godless chatter, and sword fighting over words—all of which the Bible predicts will always result in self-defeat. "If you bite and devour one another, take heed that you are not consumed by one another" (Gal 5:15).

Of course, it wasn't long before those who rose up to oppose the takeover decided that the only way to stop the political assault was to adopt some of the same secular techniques the fundamentalists were using. So this barefaced embracing of worldly weapons—by both sides—created a climate where ruthless and inconsiderate incivility took root and, to some extent, continues to infect our Baptist family to this day.

Higher Ground: The Example of Jesus

That's why I felt compelled to address the issue of worldly weapons in the Convention sermon at the annual Southern Baptist Convention meeting in Kansas City in 1984. "Higher Ground" was the title of the sermon, and its second point was "Let's turn from the muddy swamps of political coercion to the higher ground of spiritual persuasion." I reminded the messengers that by His commands and example, Jesus made it unmistakably clear that the power we are to employ in our work for Him is not political or conscriptive power, but spiritual power.

Consistently, Jesus refused to use even subtle coercion in His mission. He rejected the low ground of political maneuvering and chose instead the higher ground of spiritual persuasion. What a contrast the Gospels give us in the account of Jesus' entry into Jerusalem (Matt 21:1-11). He was not mounted on a war-horse like a Roman general, nor thundering across the battlefield in a chariot, mowing down the enemy like Pharaoh or Nebuchadnezzar. Instead, He came riding on a donkey, the epitome of meekness, patience, gentleness, and peace.

To the Roman legions stationed in Jerusalem, He must have appeared comical. A "king" entering on a donkey rather than a commander's stallion, seated on folded cloaks, not a proper saddle. His entourage made up of peasants, not soldiers. His troops brandishing palm branches, not spears. Instead of the blare of trumpets and patriotic drumbeats, He is welcomed by hymns of Hosanna. This was surely no rival of Caesar, just a toothless lion, a paper tiger. How ironic! Jesus, the Son of God, chose to enter the city as a pauper prince on a borrowed donkey.

And yet, this powerless, penniless, meek, and gentle Savior is in reality the Conqueror of the world, the King of kings, the Lord of lords. He teaches us that gentleness is royal and omnipotent, while worldly force and political coercion are ultimately feeble. The wings of the heavenly dove fly farther than the wings of Rome's eagles with their strong talons and bloody beaks.

Our Savior wept over Jerusalem, but He never besieged it, never rallied its legislature or courts to favor His cause, never formed a political coalition to advance His kingdom. Not once did He rely on a government agency or authority to advance His spiritual mission. As a recent bumper sticker put it, "Jesus didn't boycott sinners!" He preached the good news of salvation, prayed, loved, healed the sick, fed the hungry, helped the poor, and even to the point of sacrificial death, He steadfastly rejected worldly force.

During recent discussions over the public display of the Ten Commandments, Derek Davis, director of the J.M. Dawson Institute of Church-State Studies at Baylor University, pointed out that

> Jesus didn't spend His time crafting large monuments of the Ten Commandments and erecting them in places where everyone could see them. He didn't wear a Ten Commandments T-shirt or carry copies of the Commandments with Him, stopping here and there to make sure they were posted publicly for all to be reminded that the law of God was the foundation of society. Jesus' mission was not a political one but a spiritual one.[1]

Heaven's entire angelic army was at His command. With the snap of a finger, He could have brought Herod and Pilate to their knees in surrender and enthroned Himself as a king in Jerusalem, but He didn't. John 6:15 says, "Perceiving then that they were about to come and take Him by force to make Him king, Jesus withdrew again to the mountain by Himself." He came not to be an autocrat, but a servant leader.

John 9:54 says that even though James and John thought it was a great idea, Jesus would not call down fire from heaven on those who disagreed with Him. Respecting that fragile jewel called free will, Jesus refused to manipulate, coerce, or commandeer the people. He chose persuasive preaching, teaching, reasoning, and love as His weapons. He who could wither a fig tree at fifty paces with a spoken rebuke, and with one word de-fang a howling windstorm into a whimpering breeze, would not force His will on others. Jesus could have pulled the trigger of His power and with one divine laser blast vaporized the ones who nailed Him to the cross, but instead He prayed, "Father, forgive them, for they know not what they do."

In Matthew 26:52. Simon Peter drew his weapon in the garden in a foolhardy attempt to resist the soldiers who came to arrest Jesus, but Jesus rebuked him: "Put your sword back into its place, for all who take up the sword will perish by the sword." We can learn from the example of Jesus. For it may seem appropriate at times for us to enlist the civil powers of the state in our witness for Christ. But beware, that's the low road to the misty swamps. Jesus chose the higher ground of spiritual persuasion.

A Warning to Fellow Baptists

Because Baptists have been in the minority most of their history and have suffered the abuse of political majorities who used civil power as weapons, they have vigorously rejected political alliances and coercive weapons. And, historically, Baptists have been their best when they've been content to use preaching and witness and prayer and persuasion. Even when they found themselves in positions of prominence and in league with the powerful, Baptists in the past worked hard to protect the freedom of the minorities who differed from them, guaranteeing religious liberty for all.

Unfortunately, many twenty-first-century Baptists have lost sight of that historic pattern. They need to recall their proud past and preserve the distinctive biblical message: "Render unto Caesar the things that are Caesar's and unto God the things that are God's." "Not by might nor by power, but by my Spirit, says the Lord Almighty." If our Baptist forebears could warn us, they would probably say this:

> Go ahead. Engage the government as your ally. Since you and other Evangelicals are a major political force today and hold the power to influence Congress, go ahead and breech the wall of separation and bend the guarantees of religious liberty a little bit so that your faith enjoys the support of the state. It sounds like a good idea. If the sword of federal support is offered, grasp it. Use it. But watch out, Jesus said, "They that take up the sword will die by the sword."
>
> Call on Big Brother in Washington to help you witness and worship, and Big Brother will trivialize your Lord, reducing His sacred birth to nothing more than a folk festival, giving Bethlehem's manger no more significance than Santa's sleigh or Rudolph's red nose.
>
> Ask the Supreme Court to endorse your Christian faith, and they will relegate the virgin-born Jesus, the only begotten of the Father, the King of kings and Lord of lords, to the company of Frosty the Snowman and Alvin the Caroling Chipmunk.
>
> Don't forget, it's better to have enemies who know who Christ is and detest Him than political friends in high places who classify the eternal word of God with fairy tales. Entangle the church in government affairs, and the church quickly becomes nothing more than another political action group, lobbying for special interests.
>
> Some day in the future, as so often in the past, other political forces hostile to religious liberty will hold the advantage. They will have the political clout you Baptists and Evangelicals have today, and they may breech that crack you so casually made in the wall of separation, and circumvent the guarantees you brazenly bent a little bit, and they may steal away the liberty you carelessly abused. And future

generations of Americans will look back on your century and wonder what happened to that country which a Baptist musician described as "sweet land of liberty."

Have you ever studied the tragic experience of Baptists in Germany during Hitler's rise to power? We who've never lived under a repressive regime like the Third Reich should be slow to condemn, but the lessons of their failure are so timely.

Church historians describe how German Baptists, rightly concerned about immorality in their country in the 1930s, rallied behind Hitler's drive to rid society of pornography, prostitution, homosexuality, and other social sins. Deceived by the Orwellian double-speak of Nazi propaganda, and impressed with Hitler's righteous campaign against "degenerates" and his pious commitment to what he called "positive Christianity," German Baptists temporarily lost sight of their traditional antipathy toward establishment religion. They developed alliances with the government and received unprecedented privileges while other religious groups were being persecuted.

For the first time in 100 years, German Baptists enjoyed the paternal care of their government. In contrast to their forebears who had struggled as a persecuted minority, they were now the privileged ones. They dismissed the government restrictions placed on Lutheran and Evangelical congregations as divine judgment for the years they had harassed Baptist churches. So long as they remained unmolested by the authorities, these Baptists shrank from endangering their own privileged freedom by challenging the state. And they discovered too late that they were duped.

The lesson is clear. Individual believers should be involved as Christian citizens at every level of our democratic processes of government, but only to ensure that personal freedom and justice are maintained, never to secure privileged support from the state nor encourage its entanglement in religious affairs. We should steadfastly refuse to take up the sword of government alliance and political clout, and reclaim that historical legacy of separation of church and state. We must choose as Jesus did, to employ only spiritual weapons. We don't have to look to a benevolent uncle in Washington. We have an omnipotent Father in heaven!

Conclusion

It was encouraging to see newspaper columnist Cal Thomas, who is considered a strong conservative voice, calling for Christians to avoid the use of political weapons. He rightly argued that there is no biblical mandate, or expectation, for reforming the world through government. Reflecting on the death of the political organization called "The Christian Coalition," he explained why such worldly efforts fail:

> Religious politics failed the church because believers were told they could improve the morals of a nation through legislation and politics. It failed the state because time that might have been spent preaching a gospel of redemption—that would have had the collateral benefit of elevating culture—was wasted in a futile attempt to reform the unconverted.
>
> Things might have been better if, instead of sending money to the national headquarters of religious leaders and pledging allegiance to their preferred politicians, conservative Christians had been busy feeding the hungry, clothing the naked, visiting those in prison, caring for widows and orphans and—most notably absent from the movement—loving their enemies.[2]

Thomas made it clear that the separation of state and church doesn't mean Christians shouldn't be involved in the political process. They should be informed, vote intelligently, take active roles in political parties, and run for office, but they shouldn't substitute these secular strategies for spiritual ones. He reminded Christians that while political power is limited and often disappoints, the power of God is unlimited and ultimately succeeds. He concluded with a call for Christians to spend less time trying to influence Caesar, and to spend more time considering what it means to "render unto God," and to start rendering! To that we would add a strong "Amen!"

In his address at the National Prayer Breakfast in Washington in 1996, former U.S. senator from Georgia, Sam Nunn, described the situation when Jesus began his ministry 2,000 years ago. He told how the people of the day were expecting the triumphant arrival of a powerful political leader to throw off the Roman oppression and establish a new government:

> Instead, God sent His Son, a baby, born in a stable. Jesus grew up to become a peasant carpenter in a backwater town called Nazareth. He condemned sin but made it clear that He loved the sinner. He befriended beggars, prostitutes and even tax collectors while condemning the hypocrisy of those in power. He treated every individual with love and dignity and taught that we should do the same. He also put the role of government in proper perspective when He said, "Render unto Caesar that which is Caesar's and unto God that which is God's."[3]

The church will fail if it chooses to remain in the "muddy swamps of political coercion," trying to succeed using force, clever manipulation, sensationalism, politics, or other carnal weapons from the world's arsenal. Instead, God has provided the "higher ground of spiritual persuasion." That's where we find the powerful armaments of meekness, love, gentleness, persuasion, witness, and prayer. And that's where a renewed spirit of Christian civility can be born.

Jesus chose that higher ground of spiritual persuasion to carry out His mission, and so should we.

Notes

[1] Derek H. Davis, "Commandments Best Kept in Mind," *Dallas Morning News,* 8 October 2005, H4.

[2] Cal Thomas, "The Death of Religious Politics," *Dallas Morning News,* 11 December 2003, B13.

[3] Sam Nunn, "Separation of Church and State," *Washington Post,* 18 February 1996, OP/ED.

Humility,
Not Self-Promotion

One evidence of the lack of Christian civility today is a glaring absence of humility. With their emphasis on self-fulfillment and protecting one's turf, these days have rightly been dubbed "the era of narcissism." Unfortunately, this self-centered competitiveness has invaded the world of Christian leadership. Climbing the professional ladder at all costs, elbowing past others on their way to the top, competing for the chief seats—all these tactics and more are now seen among those called to serve the One who had no place to lay His head. Such behavior may be acceptable on Madison Avenue and Wall Street, but it's not acceptable on the Way of the Cross.

An ambitious frog watched with envy each year as the geese in his pond flapped their wings and flew south. He desperately wanted to take that trip with them, so he hatched a clever scheme. Persuading two of his goose friends to hold each end of a length of string in their beaks, he clamped down on the middle of the string with his strong jaws as they took off toward warmer climate. Everything was working well until he flew over a group of spectators on the ground. They were impressed as they looked up and shouted, "What a clever idea; I wonder who invented that?" Unable to resist the temptation to take credit for his ingenious scheme, the frog opened his mouth to shout, "*I* did!" His flight ended abruptly as he plummeted to the ground.

There are a lot of proud people suffering from that kind of "I" trouble today, and some of them claim to be followers of Jesus.

A faithful parishioner came to talk to her pastor about a serious spiritual problem. "I have sin in my life, pastor," she confessed. "What is it, Ms. Jones?" "It's vanity," she went on. "You know that large mirror out in the foyer? Everybody stops there on the way into church to check their hair or straighten their tie, but when I look in the mirror, I linger. I look at myself, and I can't resist saying, 'You are one gorgeous woman!'" The pastor broke in "Oh Ms. Jones," he said, "that's not vanity; that's glaucoma!"

There are a lot of proud people suffering from that kind of "I" trouble today, and some of them claim to be followers of Jesus.

After the military rescue operation in Grenada in 1983, the U.S. government awarded 8,614 decorations for bravery in action. That was a shocking revelation since only 7,000 troops were involved in the fighting. Many of the medals for bravery under fire went to bureaucrats in the Pentagon or Fort Bragg who sat behind desks and were never in danger. Government bureaucracies really know how to congratulate themselves, don't they?[1]

But we Baptists (especially those of us in Texas, I'm afraid) also have a trademark reputation for bragging. We've made an art form out of patting ourselves on the back for our churchly accomplishments. God created us with our arms out in front so we couldn't pat ourselves on the back, but we've learned how to do it anyway. We're experts at giving ourselves medals, promoting our own interests, and looking out for number one.

But the problem that threatens civility today is far more serious than "Texas bragging." During our recent Baptist denominational controversy, the struggle for control often degenerated into a shameless scrambling for the "chief seats." There were times when grown adults, acting like pouting children, whined about being left out of the process. "You've had those elected positions long enough. Now it's our turn." Leadership jobs were seen as prizes to be coveted. I personally watched as shameless manipulators blatantly plotted to oust current leaders and place themselves in high-profile posts in Baptist life. They viewed these positions as coveted "plums" rather than solemn responsibilities. Once in place, mimicking the raw greed often seen in the secular world, they began to focus on the perks of the job rather than the accountability.

It all reminded me of a *New Yorker* cartoon that happened to appear during the height of the denominational struggle. It pictured a castle surrounded by an attacking army. Inside, the occupants of the castle were reading the demands of the marauders. "It seems they want us to be out there, and they want to be in here." Apropos!

It was this absence of basic Christian humility in our Baptist family that led me to focus on humility in my sermon at the Southern Baptist Convention in 1984. Again, as with this book, the title of the Convention sermon was "Higher Ground." Its third and final point was the plea, "Let's turn from the barren plains of egotistic self-interest to the higher ground of Christlike humility."[2]

What Is Christian Humility?

We've all laughed at Yogi Berra's famous misquotation, "It ain't the heat. It's the humility!" But he's not the only person to miss the true meaning of humility. Christian humility is often misunderstood and misrepresented.

There is an earthiness about the word in English. Taken from the Latin root *humus,* which means earth or soil, "humble" literally means "of the earth." Webster defines humility as "the absence of pride or self-assertion." It's that, but much more, especially from a Christian perspective. In the New Testament, humility is expressed by the Greek word *tapeinophrosune,* usually translated "lowliness of mind." It has been called modesty or self-abasement. Humble people are free from vanity and pride; they give honor to others rather than to themselves.

Humility is also linked with the word *prautes,* which is translated "meekness" or gentleness" (Gal 5:23). At times, scholars translate *prautes* as "humility," so the two words are almost synonymous, although meekness carries the additional nuance of strength under control, like a stallion that has been tamed. All his strength is still there, but he is docile and his strength is now under control. The meek, whom Jesus said would inherit the earth, are strong, but their strength is under control and channeled for God's glory. Christian humility or meekness is "refusing to regard oneself more highly than one should or to be excessively concerned about one's welfare or reputation."[3]

Contrary to the ancient Greeks and Romans, who despised humility as a demeaning characteristic, and contrary to the misunderstanding of some people today, Christian humility is not a groveling self-depreciation. To be truly humble does not demand that we become doormats or that we imitate the timid, shrinking, apologetic Caspar Milquetoast of cartoon fame. A. W. Tozer echoed this correction:

> The meek man is not a human mouse afflicted with a sense of his own inferiority. Rather, he may be in his moral life as bold as a lion and as strong as Samson; but he has stopped being fooled about himself. He has accepted God's estimate of his own life.[4]

The truly humble flaunt neither their strengths nor their weaknesses. They acknowledge that whatever power or ability they have comes from God. Leadership guru Fred Smith explained that humility is not denying the power you have but admitting that the power comes *through* you and not *from* you. He said,

> If you deny the power you've been given, you lie. If you have a fine voice, to depreciate it is to show a lack of appreciation for it. If you've been given a talent for making money (and I believe it is a talent), then use it and be the trustee of it. If your talent is administration, then help things to happen. I don't believe that God gives any talent for irresponsibility, and that is what we're showing when we fail to recognize, appreciate, and use the talent that we have been given.[5]

One of the best definitions of humility came from the nineteenth-century missionary Andrew Murray, who understood that humility is not so much thinking less of yourself, but thinking less *about* yourself. Here is his classic definition:

> Humility is perfect quietness of heart. It is to expect nothing, to wonder at nothing that is done to me, to feel nothing done against me. It is to be at rest when nobody praises me, and when I am blamed or despised. It is to have a blessed home in the Lord, where

I can go in and shut the door, and kneel to my Father in secret, and am at peace as in a deep sea of calmness, when all around and above is trouble.[6]

How Does a Person Become Humble?

The Bible presents humility from two perspectives. First, humility is described as an inner character trait planted in the believer by the indwelling of the Holy Spirit at conversion. When Jesus comes into your life, He recreates you in His likeness, and since He is "humble in heart," He "makes" you "humble in heart" (Matt 11:29). The New Testament refers to conversion as "putting on Christ Jesus," that is, assuming His likeness (Gal 3:27). Therefore, as believers we have "put on humbleness of mind" (Col 3:12). Simon Peter described it as being "clothed with humility" (1 Pet 5:5).

So, viewed from this first perspective, humility is one of the "derived" elements of Christlikeness, deeply imbedded in a believer's personality that shows the world you're a Christian. It's one dimension of the fruit of the Spirit that inevitably flows from a transformed life. Humility, then, is not so much a virtue we struggle to develop as it is a quality we already have as born-again believers. In fact, when we focus on humility or strive too hard to "acquire" it, we're no longer humble. As one anonymous writer put it, "When we become aware of our humility, we've lost it." With this in mind, Martin Luther condemned those who "instead of being humble, are always seeking to excel in humility."[7]

Second, the Bible also presents humility in terms of intentional actions we can take to express that inner quality. Since we are by our spiritual nature humble people, we should express that quality in our daily lives. Notice Paul didn't say to the Philippian Christians, "Have this mind (of humility) in you that was in Christ Jesus." He assumed the mindset was already there, and he said, "Have this mind—*among yourselves*—which was in Christ Jesus." He was encouraging them to apply the inner quality of Christlike humility that had been planted within them at conversion. Lest they miss what that entails, he added, "Do nothing from selfishness or conceit, but in humility count others better than yourselves. Let each of you look not only to his own interests, but also to the interests of others" (Phil 2:3-5).

So, according to the Bible, humility is an inner quality of Christlikeness, but the believer is to live out that quality in daily living. What are some actions we can take to express our inner humility?

1. Do nothing from selfishness or conceit. (Phil 2:3)
2. Count others better than yourself. (Phil 2:3)
3. Look not only to your own interests, but to the interests of others. (Phil 2:4)
4. Be open and teachable like a little child. (Matt 18:4)
5. Go and sit in the lowest place. (Luke 14:10)
6. Don't think of yourself more highly than you ought to think. (Rom 12:3)
7. Be subject to one another. (Eph 5:21)
8. Don't commend yourself. (2 Cor 10:18)
9. Exhibit a life of lowliness and meekness. (Eph 4:1-2)
10. Show *agape* love which is not boastful or arrogant, and does not insist on its own way. (1 Cor 13:4)

In other words, we should adopt intentionally an attitude, a worldview that is outward not inward, unselfish not selfish. Remembering that God hates pride and arrogance, we should try to be unassuming, unostentatious, unpretentious rather than boastful, pedantic, vain, or egotistical (Prov 8:13).

As we live out in daily life the inner quality of humility, Paul reminds us of the dangers of false humility. In Colossians 2:18 and 23 he warns against "an appearance of self-abasement." The King James translation reads, "voluntary humility." Samuel Taylor Coleridge must have had Paul's caution in mind when he wrote, "And the Devil did grin, for his darling sin is pride that apes humility."[8]

The Importance of Christian Humility

Christian theologians and philosophers from every century have given a supreme position to humility as a crucial Christian virtue.

Augustine said, "Humility is the foundation of all the other virtues, hence in the soul in which this virtue does not exist there cannot be any other virtue except in mere appearance." He added, "If you ask me what is the first precept of the Christian religion, I will answer, first, second and third, humility." According to Barnabas, humility is "inward fasting." Chrysostom called it "the foundation of our philosophy."[9]

Martin Luther called humility "aptness for grace, the essence of faith." He said, "Unless a man is always humble, distrustful of himself, always fears his own understanding, passions, and will, he will be unable to stand for long without offence. Truth will pass him by."[10]

John Calvin believed humility constitutes faith because faith is the abandonment of self-confidence. He echoed Chrysostom's claim that humility is the foundation of philosophy, and he quoted approvingly Augustine's famous words in the paragraph above.[11]

Christian Humility and John the Baptist

The first man to carry the name "Baptist" was John, the forerunner of the Messiah. Jesus lauded him as the greatest man who ever lived: "Among those born of women there has risen no one greater than John the Baptist" (Matt 11:11). But John's greatness was linked not to his arrogant self-esteem, but to his genuine humility. Every reference to John the Baptist in the Bible has the tone of personal depreciation. John 1:8 says, "He was not that light, but was sent to bear witness of that light." In verse 15 John says of himself, "He who comes after me was before me. He has a higher rank than I have." He claims in verse 27, "He who comes after me is preferred before me. His sandal straps I am not worthy to unlatch."

John's enemies thought it would make him jealous when they told him in John 10 that Jesus was baptizing more people than he was. (What would some of our preachers say today if they were told that a neighboring pastor reported more baptisms than they did?) John's response was, "I must decrease; He must increase." In John 1:20 a delegation from Jerusalem asks him, "Who are you?" His reply: "I am *not* the Christ. I'm *not* the Prophet; I'm *not* even Elijah. I am a voice"—literally in the Greek language, *phone*, as in telephone—that's all, a voice.

Ask a compass, "Are you north?" No answer; it just swings its faithful arrow toward the magnetic pole and points. Ask John, "Are you the light?" No answer; he just turns his face toward Jesus and points, "Behold the Lamb of God." John made humility a sacred art form. He never filed an IRS tax return, but if he had, his "Personal Depreciation Schedule" would have been a classic!

After John's death, Jesus visited the place across the Jordan where John ministered in the early days, and He discovered that the people still remembered and admired John. They said, "John never worked a miracle, but everything he told us about Jesus was true." The Gospel then states, "And in that place many believed in Jesus" (John 10:40-42).

Isn't it a shame today when ministers become the focus of their own ministry, when self-promotion, autocratic leadership styles, and success goals become our highest priorities? Or worse, isn't it tragic when a church begins to worship its pastor instead of the Lord who called him, focusing on the herald instead of the King? No matter how great your pastor is, he's not the light, he's just a *phone*, a voice, pointing to the true light, announcing the King whose sandals none of us is worthy to unlatch.

Christian Humility and the First Disciples of Jesus

Who can forget that embarrassing incident in Mark 10:37 when James and John asked their special favor of Jesus? He had just revealed to them in graphic detail how He would soon be crucified, how the authorities would mock him, scourge him, expose him, and kill him. And do you remember how James and John responded to that solemn prediction? They said to Jesus, "Grant us to sit, one on your right hand and one at your left in your glory." Incredible!

In fact, it seems Jesus was always catching the disciples at each other's throats about who was the greatest. So Jesus gave them a lesson in polite civility: "When you are invited, go and sit in the lowest place, so that when your host comes he may say to you, 'Friend, go up higher.' For everyone who exalts himself will be humbled, and he who humbles himself will be exalted" (Luke 14:10).

He called on His disciples to humble themselves like a little child. He told them that the first shall be last and the last first. If they wanted to be great, they should become servants of all, and to illustrate that seeming contradiction, He washed the disciples' feet (see John 13:5). He said, "Take my yoke upon you and learn from me, for I am gentle and humble in heart" (Matt 11:29). The moment we imitate James and John in reaching for greatness through self-promotion, or the moment we imitate the Pharisees in seeking the chief seats, in that moment, ironically, we're actually going lower. We're bogged down in the lowlands, in the barren plains of egotistic self-interest. But the moment we imitate Jesus, let his lowliness of mind be our example, in that moment, ironically, we're actually climbing to the higher ground of Christlike humility.

While serving as president at Southwestern Seminary, I had a luncheon for a famous television evangelist who was often introduced as "the next Billy Graham." His secretary called to ask if I would please arrange for a private room. She said the evangelist was so well-known that he could never eat in a public restaurant. His fans would mob him and interrupt his meal. It sounded a little presumptuous, but I followed her suggestion for privacy.

However, I couldn't help but remember the time when I entertained the *real* Billy Graham. It was during his crusade in Atlanta years earlier. The crusade committee asked me to arrange a golf game and a luncheon for Dr. Graham on a Monday. I was really excited. The best golf courses were closed on Mondays, so I pulled strings and enlisted the famous golf pro at the Atlanta Country Club, Davis Love, Sr., to open his course just for Billy Graham and the rest of our foursome. Then, I planned an elegant luncheon in one of Atlanta's prestigious private clubs.

But when I called Dr. Graham to tell him my plans, do you know what *he* asked me to arrange? After hearing my suggestions, he (not his secretary) thanked me, but humbly asked if we might make some changes. He would rather play at a public golf course and eat at a public cafeteria near his hotel! I couldn't believe it.

When I picked him up, Dr. Graham wore an old golf cap and dark sunglasses, and we played almost unnoticed on one of the sorriest golf courses in Atlanta, right under the flight path of the airport. Then, believe it or not, we pushed our trays through the line at Morrison's Cafeteria for lunch. As you can imagine, I was fighting an irresistible urge to point to this man in the golf cap and sunglasses and to say to everybody, "Do you know who this is? Do you know who I'm with?" No one recognized him until halfway through the meal, and he greeted that one nervous intruder graciously and kindly. The contrast between these two men was stark. One walked on the barren plains of self-interest; the other walked on higher ground.

What do you think Jesus, who rebuked James and John for their petty self-promotion, would say about the blatant scramble for denominational chief seats during the recent denominational controversy? "We've been left out. It's our turn to be elected. Put us on the boards and committees. Give us the prime positions." It sounds a lot like the egotistic self-interest of the Sons of Thunder, doesn't it?

When shrewd brokers of power manipulate a denomination's democratic processes in order to promote themselves, they've slipped from God's high ground to the barren plains of selfish ambition and conceit. And the Bible says, "Let nothing be done through selfish ambition or conceit, but in lowliness of mind let each esteem another better than himself " (Phil 2:3).

Did you hear about the two hikers who encountered a grizzly bear on the trail? One of them quickly sat down, took off his heavy hiking boots, reached in his backpack, and slipped on his running shoes. His companion said, "What are you doing? You know you can't outrun that bear." The other replied, "I don't have to outrun the bear. I just have to outrun *you!*"

But we're not supposed to be outrunning each other; we're supposed to be standing together *with* each other against the real enemies—principalities and powers and the ruler of darkness and the hosts of wickedness in high places. We don't need "king of the mountain" competition today; we need compassionate cooperation.

Like Jesus' first disciples, we present-day followers need to remember that God didn't put us here to see through each other; He put us here to see each other through.

> All of you be submissive to one another, and clothe yourselves, all of you, with humility toward one another, for God opposes the proud, but gives grace to the humble. Therefore humble yourselves under the mighty hand of God, that in due time, He may exalt you. (1 Pet 5:5-6)

Christian Humility and the Early Church

The lack of humility among these first disciples of Jesus must also have been a problem years later in some of the early churches. The Apostle Paul repeatedly repudiated boasting in his letters. To the Roman Christians he wrote, "For by the grace given to me I bid every one among you not to think of himself more highly than he ought to think. Love one another with brotherly affection. Outdo one another in showing honor" (Rom 12:3, 10).

To the church members in Philippi he wrote, "Do nothing from selfishness or conceit, but in humility count others better than yourselves. Let each of you look not only to your own interests, but also to the interests of others" (Phil 2:3-4). As followers of Jesus, they ought to imitate His humility. Paul reinforced his advice by adding the poetic words in verses 6-11. They are written in the literary form called a *chiasmus*, and they comprise one of the mountain peaks of high Christology in the New Testament.

> Who, being in very nature, God,
> > did not consider equality with God
> > something to be grasped,
> But made himself nothing,
> > taking the very nature of a servant,
> > being made in human likeness.

And being found in appearance as a man
>He humbled Himself and became obedient to death—
>even death on a cross!
Therefore God exalted Him to the highest place
>and gave Him the name
>that is above every name.
That at the name of Jesus
>every knee should bow
>in heaven and on earth and under the earth,
And every tongue confess
>that Jesus is Lord
>to the glory of God the Father. (NIV)

The apostle was especially careful to condemn intellectual pride. It's ironic—even paradoxical—that Paul placed high priority on learning but at the same time devalued knowledge. "Knowledge puffs up. . . . If any one imagines that he knows something, he does not yet know as he ought to know. . .therefore let anyone who thinks that he stands, take heed lest he fall." "I know nothing except Christ and Him crucified" (1 Cor 8:1, 10:12).

He encouraged believers to be learners not knowers. Of course, experiential certainty is God's gift of grace. Experientially, we can know we're saved. We can have a profound inner certainty of the truthfulness of Scripture and of the great basic convictions of our faith about God, Jesus, the Holy Spirit, creation, redemption, salvation, *etc.* But the fact is that even though we've been redeemed, we're still sinful creatures whose intellects are limited by our imperfect humanity. We are to come to God not as proud know-it-alls but like little children, teachable and ready to learn.

I'm grateful to Baylor University professor Roger Olson for making distinctions among *Dogma, Doctrine,* and *Opinions.* Dogma are those basic, first-order convictions referred to above. The Christian community agrees with these, and there is little argument about them. Next, there are doctrines. These are the specific beliefs that identify different denominations. We Baptists, for example, hold to certain unique doctrines that we believe are important—the priesthood of each believer, once saved always saved, baptism by immersion, liberty of conscience, separation of church and state, and others. We would die for these convictions, but we don't suggest that those who don't hold them are infidels. Third, there are opinions. These include such things as worship styles, millennial theories, and the role of women in the church. Serious problems arise when someone tries to elevate personal opinions to the level of doctrine or even dogma.

It's unseemly for a Christian to claim to have all the answers or know all the right opinions. Unfortunately, in the heat of discussions, a debater will boldly claim that, without any shadow of doubt, his position is the only true one. I heard one astonished participant in a debate say, "I wish I could be as sure about anything as that brother is about everything!" Benjamin Franklin said we should all be willing to doubt a little of our own infallibility!

In humility, we must always listen politely to each other's opinions, be genuinely open to truth wherever it appears, and be willing to acknowledge that our opinions could be wrong. Depending on the God of truth to illumine our minds, we must always be humble "learners" not proud "knowers."

The Bible warns that the human desire for absolute intellectual certainty can become idolatry. "Knowledge puffs up. . . . If anyone imagines that he knows something, he does not yet know as he ought to know" (1 Cor 8:1-2). If we knew all the answers, we wouldn't need God! We must always stand in awe at the mysteries of God, the vast ambiguities, the complexities and nuances of truth, the unfathomable depths of His word, which even at our scholarly best we can't fully grasp or unravel.

In discussing intellectual humility, Martin Luther said, "Unless you mistrust your own understanding, truth will pass you by." He pointed out that God's grace and truth come not to the know-it-all, but to teachable people like Mary who "sat at Jesus' feet and listened humbly to His words. She was a seeker after truth who remembered that Jesus said, 'Take my yoke upon you and learn from me, for I am gentle and lowly in heart, and you will find rest for your souls.' (Matt 11:29)."[12]

Conclusion

Let's remember that we're people into whose lives the Lord Jesus Christ has come to dwell. He is the perfect personification of humility, and one way we can prove we belong to Him is to demonstrate Christlike characteristics. Let's reclaim that quality of Christlike meekness so lacking in our uncivil society. Let's turn from the barren plains of egotistic self-interest to the higher ground of Christian humility. That would give our culture a welcomed boost toward civility.

Notes

[1] David H. Hackworth, *About Face: The Odyssey of an American Warrior* (New York: Simon & Schuster, 1990) 675. (This news story also recorded in *Time Magazine*, 9 April 1984).

[2] See the discussion in the preface.

[3] Millard Erickson, *Concise Dictionary of Christian Theology* (Grand Rapids: Baker, 1994) 78.

[4] A. W. Tozer, *The Pursuit of God* (Camp Hill: Christian Publications, 1998) 103.

[5] Fred Smith, "Leadership," *Leadership Journal* (Winter 1998), <www.Christianitytoday.com>

[6] This passage from Murray is often quoted, but its source in Murray's writings is unknown. Virginia Ely, *I Quote: A Collection of Ancient and Modern Wisdom & Inspiration* (New York: George W. Stewart Publishers, 1947) 1666-7.

[7] Walter A. Elwell, *Evangelical Dictionary of Theology* (Grand Rapids: Baker, 1984) 537.

[8] Samuel Taylor Coleridge, *Poetical Works of S. T. Coleridge* (London: W. Pickering, 1835) 83-87.

[9] Ibid.

[10] Ibid.

[11] John Calvin, *Institutes of the Christian Religion*, vol. 2, bk. 2, ch. 2, pt. 2. (Albany: Ages Software, n.d.) 27.

[12] Elwell, *Evangelical Dictionary.*

Biblical Forgiveness, Not Grudges

Following the unpleasantness surrounding my dismissal (involuntary retirement) from the presidency of Southwestern Seminary, I was sometimes asked the question, "Can't you just forgive them and move on?" It's an appropriate inquiry because the world is full of victims of unspeakable injustice who harbored their resentment year after year until it became an obsession, robbing them of happiness and constructive productivity. Can't you just forgive them and move on?

My answer to the question is, "Yes. As a matter of fact I have long ago forgiven those who unjustly without warning or warrant fired me from the presidency and locked me out of my office. I have forgiven them for the tsunami of hurt, anguish, financial losses, embarrassment, and personal disruption of my life their actions caused. With God's help, I long ago got over the anger and have gone on with my life."

But there's more to forgiveness than that. For example, I've discovered that I can't forgive them for the damage they did to the seminary—to its young students who were preparing to follow their calling into ministry, to the outstanding faculty and staff who had invested so much of their lives in Southwestern, to the thousands of graduates around the world who were proud of their seminary heritage, to the generous donors who had enabled the school to become one of the best, to the citizens of Fort Worth who took pride in their community asset, to the Baptist family who had birthed and nurtured this institution for a hundred years, to the fellowship of theological education colleagues in North American and around the globe—and for the damage they did to our denomination and to the Kingdom of

God in general. I can't even forgive them for what their actions did to my family. All of these suffered immensely, and I have not forgiven them for that immeasurable damage their actions caused.

Why can't I forgive them? Because it is neither my responsibility nor my prerogative to do it. That forgiveness is between the guilty ones and the injured ones. If a man steals $100 from me, I can and should be willing to forgive him. But if someone steals $100 from you, I have no right to say, "Don't worry about it. I've forgiven him." That's your responsibility—not mine. I can't forgive people for what they do to somebody else. To claim to do that would be presumptuous. Only God has that power to forgive what people do to others. I can only forgive what is done to me.

This is what Fyodor Dostoevsky must have had in mind in *The Brothers Karamazov* when he had Ivan saying, "And above all, I don't want the mother to embrace the torturer whose dogs tore her son apart! She dare not forgive him! She has no right to forgive him! Let her, if she will, forgive him her own suffering, her own extreme anguish as a mother, but she has no right to forgive the suffering of her mutilated child."[1]

When a Jewish man named Simon Wiesenthal was in a Nazi concentration camp, he was led to the bedside of a dying German soldier. The soldier confessed that he took part in the killing of Jews and wanted Wiesenthal to forgive him before he died. Wiesenthal refused because he believed he had no right to forgive the soldier of what he did to other people. He imagined meeting in the afterlife Jews who were killed and hearing them say, "Who gave you the right to forgive our murderers?"[2]

So forgiveness is not always the simple process it seems at first to be—especially forgiveness from a biblical perspective. A precise analysis of what we often view as simple forgiveness shows us just how complex it is.

There are several scientific studies underway around the world that are attempting to provide that precise analysis by unraveling the mysteries and complexities of forgiveness. One of these, for example, is the Campaign for Forgiveness Research at Virginia Commonwealth University headed by Professor Everett Worthington.[3] It has funded thirty-eight forgiveness projects exploring the psychological and physiological dynamics of human forgiveness. But forgiveness doesn't lend itself to such objective intellectual analysis. In the midst of his project, Professor Worthington's seventy-six-year-old widowed mother was murdered by a teenage burglar. When he heard the police description of what happened to his mother, forgiveness was the last thing on his mind. He pointed to a baseball bat in the room and said, "I wish whoever did that was here. I would beat his brains out!" (So much for scientific analysis!)

The professor had encountered, like we all do, one of the numerous complex dilemmas of forgiveness. We can try to objectify forgiveness and theoretically analyze it, but when we are hit with a real life tragedy and we honestly attempt to forgive, we run into some stubborn questions.

- Can one person forgive an evildoer for what he did to another person?
- Should forgiveness be unconditional, or must the guilty one confess, repent, and ask for forgiveness?
- Is forgiveness always an individual act, or can institutions or groups forgive? Pope John Paul II publicly forgave the man who nearly killed him in 1981 within three days after the assassination attempt. But when Pope John Paul II asked Jews to forgive the Roman Catholic Church's wrongs committed throughout its history, was that appropriate or even possible?
- Can someone today repent and ask forgiveness for sins others committed years earlier? On the sixtieth anniversary of Japan's defeat in World War II, their prime minister apologized for "the huge damage and suffering" caused by Japan's military aggression. But representatives of other Asian countries refused to accept the apology or forgive, demanding compensation and other forms of retribution.
- Can institutions or a group, like the Jews, forgive another group, or can only individuals forgive?
- Is it possible to pray for one's enemies, forgive them, and at the same time try to prevent them from doing further damage—even

by killing them? Is there a difference between vengeance and justice?

- Are national actions like the Marshall Plan and similar alliances with Germany and Japan after World War II examples of a kind of "political forgiveness"?
- Does full forgiveness require reconciliation or a reestablishment of a positive relationship with the one forgiven?
- How can we be sure that we have truly forgiven someone?
- Is there a difference between forgiving and excusing someone?
- Is forgiveness possible or even appropriate in the face of a heinous crime like Timothy McVeigh's bombing in Oklahoma or Hitler's holocaust?

God's word sheds some distinctive light on the complexity of forgiveness raised by these and other questions.

1. *Biblical forgiveness is not forgetting what happened.* The popular admonition "forgive and forget" is not a biblical concept. True, the prophet Jeremiah rejoiced in the fact that God not only forgives, but "remembers our sins no more!" (Jer 31:34). But we creatures are not able to wipe our memories clear of past injustices. The more we try to forget, the more we remember. In fact, an important element in responsible ethical living *is* appropriate resentment at injustice, oppression, and other wrongs. Anger is okay. The trouble comes when we nurture our anger and allow it to degenerate into smoldering hostility that seeks vengeance or retribution.

In his book *The Angry Christian*, Andrew Lester declares, "I believe that *not being angry* at evil in all of its manifestations is sinful. In these circumstances, anger is a moral response." He quotes Elie Wiesel's belief that God has given us an important eleventh commandment: "Thou shalt not stand idly by!"[4] The Bible implies that it's okay to be angry about the bad things that happen to us, to resent them. It not only says it's okay, but actually commands us, "Be angry but do not sin; do not let the sun go down on your anger" (Eph 4:26). Our example in this is Jesus who Himself demonstrated a righteous indignation and anger at wrongdoing (Mark 3:5, 10:14; John 2:13-16).

But while we remember the wrongdoing, we don't have to dwell on the past or be enslaved by those memories. After an interval of seething and fuming, we need to get over it. As the years go by, the pain diminishes and the anger fades, but forgiveness is not forgetting. In fact, remembering the hurt can help us avoid becoming victims again and can lead to preventative measures that may help others avoid similar tragedies.

2. *Biblical forgiveness is not trivializing what happened as though it really didn't matter.* Transgression is always serious, and even when it's forgiven, its consequences often continue into eternity. To pretend the evil never happened or to ignore or overlook the gravity of the bad deed is never appropriate. That would lead to pseudo-forgiveness.

In his article "The Other Side of Rage" in *Christian Century*, Garrett Keizer pointed out that after His resurrection, Jesus still had the holes in His hands and His side. His forgiveness of those who nailed Him to the cross did not require that He hide the evidence nor minimize the enormity of His hurt.[5]

3. *Biblical forgiveness is not the same as excusing someone.* When someone injures us accidentally or out of ignorance, we tend to excuse them, overlooking their unintentional act. Forgiveness is more serious and is more appropriately applied to those who commit intentional injuries or whose gross negligence is a serious and costly lapse of responsibility (i.e., a drunken driver). When we accidentally stumble into someone, we usually say, "Excuse me," not "Please forgive me." True forgiveness is not an issue in a situation like that.

(Will Rogers once said that Americans are very generous people and will forgive almost any weakness, with the possible exception of stupidity. Theodore Roosevelt quoted a famous "straight-shooting" Texan who admitted he might, in the end, pardon a man who shot him on purpose, but that he would surely never forgive one who did it accidentally!)

But isn't it true that on the cross, Jesus prayed, "Father, forgive them for they know not what they do" (Luke 23:34)? Yes, but some interpreters remind us that the word Jesus used here, *aphes,* can also mean "let them alone, allow them, don't stop them." It's the same word He used in Matthew 19:14: "Let (*aphes*) the little children come to me, and do not hinder them." Could it be that Jesus was saying, "Father, let (*aphes*) them continue, don't stop them; they know not what they do"? Some have translated the verse, "Father *excuse* them...."[6]

Even if He did have forgiveness in mind when He asked His Father to "*aphes*" them, their ignorance and His forgiveness would still not save them. They still would have had to repent and accept that forgiveness to be reconciled to God.

4. *Biblical forgiveness is acknowledging the wickedness of what happened but choosing to pardon and not punish the transgressor.* Forgiveness is looking at the wrong and the wrongdoer squarely in the face, pointing the finger of blame, and then choosing to let go of the bitterness and the vengeance that is eating at the heart of the victim. In a lecture at Southwestern Seminary, Lewis Smedes pointed out, "Forgiveness is surrendering the sacred rite to get even." It is arbitrarily deciding not to punish the transgressor, not to hold a grudge, not to take revenge, balance the scales, get our "pound of flesh," or wish them ill.

The most often used word in the New Testament for forgiveness is *aphiami,* which means to send away, to abandon, to give up a debt. English translations have added, "to give up resentment, to stop being angry with, to give up claims to punish or exact penalties, to cancel, to overlook."

Forgiveness cancels the debt the transgressor owes to you. We have a built-in conviction that the scales of justice must be balanced and that the wrongs done must in some way be paid for before there can be forgiveness. Most of us have a natural hunger for getting even. But the biblical model calls for the wronged person to place the ultimate outcome of justice in God's hands and choose to live, if necessary, with the scales unbalanced. While just punishment for breaking the law is necessary, biblical forgiveness calls for the injured party to cancel the debt when the wrongdoer acknowledges the wrong and asks for forgiveness.

In all honesty, when we've been maligned, it's very difficult not to rejoice when the guilty one is injured or experiences tragedy. The feeling is they got what they deserved. But true forgiveness actually wishes good for the perpetrator. The Bible commands us to love our enemies. The word for love is *agape*, and it does not mean a warm feeling of affection for someone. Actually, *agape* love is not a feeling at all. It is an attitude of unselfish regard you deliberately choose to take toward other people—even those who despitefully use you. When you *"agape"* someone, you wish the best for them; you desire good things to happen to them. When He commanded us to love our enemies, God knew we couldn't grit our teeth and conjure up an emotion of warm affection toward those who have hurt us, but we could deliberately choose not to retaliate. We can intentionally adopt an attitude of open, unselfish concern for them and wish them well. That's *agape* love, and that's true forgiveness.

5. *Biblical forgiveness is conditional.* The Bible is consistent in its claim that God's forgiveness, while gracious and complete, is always conditional. We must acknowledge our sins and repent, that is, turn from our sins, before God's forgiveness can take effect. "*If* we confess our sins, He is faithful and just, and will forgive our sins and cleanse us from all unrighteousness" (1 John 1:9). "*If* my people who are called by my name will humble themselves, and pray and seek my face, and turn from their wicked ways, then I will hear from heaven, and will forgive their sin and heal their land" (2 Chron 7:14).

Since God's forgiveness is conditional, it seems logical that our forgiveness of others also has a conditional element. The guilty party must be willing to confess, repent, and ask forgiveness before the full effect of forgiveness can be achieved. I've come to understand that full forgiveness is conditional, that while I may have done all that is expected of me in forgiving, forgiveness is not fully complete until the wrongdoers acknowledge the wrong, repent, and accept my forgiveness. There is no possibility of complete forgiveness when someone persists in committing atrocities. L. Gregory Jones, dean of Duke University Divinity School, echoes that concept: "In the absence of repentance, it would be cheap and foolhardy to talk about forgiveness in its fullest understanding."[7]

On the other hand, however, Lewis B. Smedes argues that forgiveness should be *un*conditional. He attempts to prove his point by reminding us that it's possible to forgive a person who is dead and therefore unable to repent. But I believe forgiveness does not reach its full effect until the offending party acknowledges the wrong and repents and seeks forgiveness. Something is missing from full forgiveness without this conditional element. I can unilaterally forgive the fundamentalists who unjustly fired me without regard to their attitudes or present actions, and in so doing I have fulfilled my responsibility. But that forgiveness has not reached the ultimate conclusion until they acknowledge their wrongdoing and either ask for or accept that forgiveness. Only then can the full effect of forgiveness be completed and lead to some sort of reconciliation.

6. *Biblical forgiveness is not reconciliation.* Lewis Smedes does make a helpful distinction between forgiveness and reconciliation that he says *is* conditional. There can be forgiveness, he argues, without reconciliation, but there cannot be reconciliation without forgiveness. In other words, he claims a person can forgive another even if there is no repentance, but there can be no reconciliation between the injured and the injurer until there is an acknowledgement of the wrong, repentance for it, an expression of regret, and a request to be forgiven.

I can forgive those who wronged me even if they don't acknowledge their wrong and ask forgiveness, even though the full cycle of that forgiveness is not realized until they do. But there can be no reconciliation or a restoring of relationship with those responsible for the transgression until they admit what they did was wrong and ask forgiveness. If the offender remains unrepentant and unchanged, then reconciliation is impossible. Reconciliation also requires a renewal of trust, and sometimes that's difficult if not impossible. But without that change and without trust, reconciliation becomes no more than an armed truce with both parties waiting to resume hostilities.[8]

So, having forgiven the wrongdoers, I have neither the desire nor the right to demand or coerce their response of repentance. That response, which might lead to reconciliation, is now up to them.

It should be noted, however, that God's forgiveness is unique. When we repent and turn to God in faith, not only are we forgiven, but at the same time, our broken relationship with God is restored. "Now in Christ Jesus you who once were far off have been brought near in the blood of Christ...that He might reconcile us both to God in one body through the cross, thereby bringing the hostility to an end" (Eph 2:13, 16). So God's conditional forgiveness simultaneously brings reconciliation.

7. *Biblical forgiveness is supernatural and miraculous.* Jesus said, "If your brother sins, rebuke him, and if he repents, forgive him; and if he sins against you seven times in a day, and turns to you seven times and says 'I repent,' you must forgive him" (Luke 17:3-4). That's not easy! No wonder the next verse says, "Lord, Increase our faith!" Forgiveness is not for wimps! As Laurence Sterne put it, "Only the brave know how to forgive. . . . A coward never forgave; it's not in his nature." So forgiveness is not natural; it's supernatural. It's a grace gift the good Lord enables you give to the person who wronged you.

When the Gospel writers recorded the resurrection of Jesus, they also added the moving account of how the risen Lord forgave Peter for his cowardly denial. Recording these two events together implies that like resurrection, forgiveness is also miraculous. Forgiveness is a transcendental superhuman act of creation, bringing something entirely new and dynamic to a sterile dead-end situation. It is an act of grace that changes things. It can only be done by trusting in the God who raises the dead and whose resurrection power can enable victims to pardon those who hurt them.

8. *Biblical forgiveness is motivated by God's forgiveness of us.* There could be no stronger motivation to forgive than the fact that God will not forgive us if we don't forgive others! Jesus said, "If you forgive men their trespasses, your heavenly Father also will forgive you; but if you do not forgive men their trespasses neither will your Father forgive

your trespasses" (Matt 6:14-15). After relating the parable of the unforgiving servant who was punished by his lord, Jesus said, "So also my heavenly Father will do to every one of you, if you do not forgive your brother from your heart" (Matt 18:32-35). He also said, "And whenever you stand praying, forgive, if you have anything against any one; so that your Father also who is in heaven may forgive you your trespasses" (Mark 11:25). In the model prayer, He added, "And forgive us our debts as we also have forgiven our debtors" (Matt 6:12). "Forgive and you shall be forgiven" (Luke 6:37). The Apostle Paul put it another way: "Be kind to one another, tenderhearted, forgiving one another, as God in Christ forgave you" (Eph 4:32). "If anyone has a complaint against another, forgiving each other; as the Lord has forgiven you, so you also must forgive" (Col 3:13).

These passages teach that an unforgiving spirit blocks God's forgiveness of our sins. Since our ultimate need is to be forgiven by God, we'd better be concerned about any situation that makes it certain God will not forgive! That's strong motivation to forgive others!

9. *Biblical forgiveness acknowledges our solidarity with all sinful humanity.* True forgiveness must begin with a humble admonition of our own lack of innocence. We acknowledge that we too are sinners and need God's forgiveness. That leads us to recognize the wrongdoer's humanity. When injured, we tend to caricature the guilty one, define him or her totally in terms of the wrong they did. But authentic forgiveness allows us to see the person as another human being—complex, weak, confused, bitter, fragile—not all that different from us. We discover circumstances in the other person's life that may have led to the meanness. Those circumstances don't excuse the evil actions, but they do help us understand the perpetrator as a human being. We are forced to say, "There but for the grace of God go I! If God can forgive me, then I should try to forgive others."

Richard Neuhaus, a former Lutheran minister who is now a priest in the Roman Catholic Church, claims that not forgiving another blocks the cycle of forgiveness to yourself. We must all admit we are sinners who fully deserve to be condemned. That means you have to be generous (even promiscuous, according to Neuhaus) in being gracious with others.

10. *Biblical forgiveness usually takes time.* Just to say "I forgive" is not enough; it usually entails an extended process. Just before his death, C. S. Lewis wrote, "I think I have at last forgiven the cruel schoolmaster who so darkened my youth. I had done it many times before, but this time I think I have really done it." Maybe, had he lived longer, he would have had to do it again.[9] God can forgive instantly; we usually need time, and the deeper the wound, the longer the time needed.[10] Sometimes that process involves forgiving yourself for tolerating injustice or being duped by the wrongdoer. Sometimes the process is helped along by a sense of humor, not taking ourselves too seriously, and laughing at some features of our misfortune. There were some comical missteps in the actions of the hardliners on Southwestern's board that led to my firing. As we dealt with the sadness of the event, an occasional laugh helped smooth the road to forgiveness.

11. *Biblical forgiveness is liberating.* Psychology has shown that holding a grudge, nurturing hatred, kindling bitterness toward others—no matter how deserving they may be of your scorn—is self-defeating. Its corrosive acid can injure your health and rob you of peace and happiness. On the other hand, to forgive, to pardon, helps heal the hurt.

When Jesus commands us to forgive, it is in part for our own good. Forgiveness has a way of cauterizing our wounds, lowering our blood pressure, and diminishing our ulcers. Studies like the one in the March 2004 issue of *Psychological Science* show that unforgiving thoughts trigger stress responses such as higher blood pressure and faster heart rates, while forgiving thoughts result in milder responses.

Forgivers come to see themselves as active agents rather than helpless victims. When they take the initiative to forgive, they break the power the wrongdoer has over them and experience the exhilarating feeling of freedom! But in spite of the physiological and psychological benefits, we must see forgiveness as something more than therapeutic. The motive for forgiveness must be more than a self-centered desire for good health.

12. *Biblical forgiveness doesn't have to be perfect.* Another liberating feature of authentic forgiveness is that we aren't expected to be perfect at it. We work at it. We try. We do our best with God's help. But we must remember "God is the only professional expert at forgiveness; we're just poor amateur duffers trying to treat others as He treats us."[11] Nevertheless, as those amateur forgivers keep on trying, they are making an enormous contribution to the crusade to restore civility in our national life and in our church life.

Notes

[1] Fyodor Dostoevsky, *The Brothers Karamazov* (New York: Oxford Press, 1994) 307.

[2] Richard P. Lord, "Do I Have to Forgive?" *Christian Century* (9 October 1991): 902.

[3] Larry B. Stammer, "McVeigh Execution," *Los Angeles Times*—quoted in *Fort Worth Star Telegram,* 11 June 2001, C3.

[4] Andrew D. Lester, *The Angry Christian* (Louisville: Westminster John Knox Press, 2003) 207.

[5] Garrett Keizer, "The Other Side of Rage," *Christian Century* (31 July-13 August 2002): p. 27.

[6] Jeanne Safer, *Forgiving and Not Forgiving* (New York: Avon Books, 1999) 45.

[7] Quoted by L. Gregory Jones in *USA Today,* 10 December 2001.

[8] Robert D. Enright, *Forgiveness Is a Choice* (Washington: American Psychological Association, 2001) 31.

[9] Lewis Smedes, *Forgive and Forget* (New York: Pocket Books, 1984) 127.

[10] Smedes, *The Art of Forgiveness* (New York, Ballantine Books, 1996) 178.

[11] Smedes, "Keys to Forgiving," *Christianity Today* (3 December 2001): 73.

Respecting the Minority, Not Majoritarianism

Like so many in our harsh, bad-mannered society, Pennsylvania pastor Jay Geisler grew weary of the way fellow Christians were mimicking secular incivility. He was especially troubled by the way Christians were squabbling over political ideology rather than dealing with real problems like poverty and hopelessness in the neighborhood around his St. Stephen Episcopal Church. So he contacted Call to Renewal, one of several groups trying to restore civility and courtesy to our national life and draw Americans together. He wanted to do something because he realized polarization was tearing apart not only churches but our country as well. He said, "Each side wants winner-take-all. We don't seem to want to see win-win anymore."[1]

A surprising and often overlooked element in our epidemic of incivility is the rise of what is being called the "Winner-take-all Society." Its most obvious expression is in the world of economics. According to economists such as Robert H. Frank and Philip J. Cook, this winner-take-all mentality that rewards the highly talented performers, athletes, coaches, and other celebrities and disparages those with average abilities has troubling negative results. Winner-take-all markets have increased the disparity between rich and poor.

For example, Disney chairman Michael Eisner topped the 1993 *Business Week* chart of America's highest-paid executives, his $203 million in earnings roughly 10,000 times that of the lowest-paid Disney employee. "During the last two decades, the top 1 percent of U.S. earners captured more than 40 percent of the country's total earnings growth, one of the largest shifts any society has endured without a revolution or military defeat."[2]

The winner-take-all society also affects the field of higher education. The most talented college students are enrolled in a small set of elite institutions, making it more difficult for "late bloomers" to find a productive niche in life. This relentless emphasis on coming out on top—the best-selling book, the blockbuster film, the Super Bowl winner—has molded our discourse in ways that many find deeply troubling.[3]

In politics, this winner-take-all culture is sometimes called "majoritarianism" or even "ochlocracy." The founders of our country recognized there was a potential danger in their new democracy of what they called "the tyranny of the majority." Alexis de Tocqueville in his book *Democracy in America* (1831) warned about this danger as did John Stuart Mill in On *Liberty* (1859). Even Thomas Jefferson once said, "A democracy is nothing more than mob rule (Ochlocracy), where fifty-one percent of the people may take away the rights of the other forty-nine."[4]

Granted, in spite of this potential danger, a democracy is still the desired form of governance for a nation, or—as Baptists have practiced it—for a denominational convention or a local church congregation. Decisions made by majority vote in a democracy avoid the opposite danger of the "tyranny of the minority." But those enjoying the benefits of a free democratic form of governance must always beware of raw majoritarianism, the "tyranny of the majority."[5]

Early American patriots understood this threat. James Madison, the fourth president of the United States, warned that motivated by self-interest, a majority might be ignorant of or indifferent to the concerns of the minority. A politically dominant group, for example, might decide to name one religion a state religion and declare that other faiths are illegal.

In our United States democracy, the Constitution serves as a safeguard to avoid the tyranny of the majority. That's why its shapers made it difficult to amend the Constitution—a simple representative majority cannot do it. The separation of powers in our three branches of government is another precautionary measure that allows our democratic process to work without oppression from the majority.

In spite of the danger, Madison believed that even a self-interested majority can govern fairly if it cooperates with the minority. Actually, cooperation might even serve the self-interest of the majority because of the principle of reciprocity. The majority could become a minority in the future, so it would be in their best interest to practice the Golden Rule in their relationship with the present minority! If a political majority rules but does not dominate, and instead cooperates with the minority in a fair system of mutually beneficial collaboration, they are sometimes designated a "Madisonian Majority."[6]

Based on the philosophy behind the little book *All I Really Need to Know I Learned in Kindergarten* the cure for raw majoritarianism is to practice the elementary rules of civility and compassion: play fair, take turns, encourage everyone to play, work for consensus, and do unto others as you would have them do unto you.

Southern Baptists under their current fundamentalist leaders appear to have rejected the principle of fairness to minority voters and are practicing a majoritarian policy of total defeat of the minority opposition. In practice, at least, the prevailing philosophy of those who won the votes in various SBC meetings is "winner-take-all."

During the last twenty-five years, these ultraconservative leaders have systemically narrowed the circle of what they consider orthodox participants by ousting anyone who resisted their takeover effort. Their revision of the *1963 Baptist Faith and Message* took another step in this direction. Its stricter interpretations are intended to exclude the minority rather than unite members of the Baptist family. The revised document has fostered division within and among congregations rather than drawing the family together in cooperation. When the SBC recently voted to withdraw from affiliation with the Baptist World Alliance, they pushed the winner-take-all philosophy even further.

Following this divisive separation from Baptists around the world, the editor of *Baptists Today* reported an incident at a press conference:

A reporter for a large city newspaper asked me: "Why do Southern Baptists have this scorched-earth approach to everything?" One answer to that question is found in the comments of an SBC spokesman who told Religion News Service; "For the most part, we don't do ecumenism because you usually have to give up some doctrinal beliefs or ignore or emphasize others to work with folks that really aren't on the same path, share the same doctrines, the same beliefs—particularly about salvation."

That explains a lot. For current Southern Baptist leaders, cooperation and open conversation are wrongly equated with compromising convictions.[7]

Following a disagreement in meetings of the SBC's International Mission Board this year, the member from Oklahoma, Wade Burleson, expressed on his Internet blog some concerns about decisions being made by the board. According to Burleson, he did not break confidentiality policies or distort the facts, but merely voiced in a reasoned and careful manner his alternative viewpoint with its attendant apprehensions. The SBC leaders took exception to his comments and asked the Convention in its next session to remove him from the board. Burleson, who had been a loyal supporter of the new SBC leadership, explained that the underlying issue in his dispute with trustees is the growing division among conservative Southern Baptists over freedom of conscience:

> Are we going to continue to narrow the parameters of cooperation in our Convention by tightly controlling trustee boards and agencies to the point that that those who disagree on minor doctrinal issues are excluded from service? Are we going to allow principled dissent?[8]

The SBC has practiced majoritarianism not only by attempts to silence minority dissent, but they have also belittled the historical Baptist ideal of the separation of church and state. In its place, the current SBC leaders have substituted an unprecedented strategy of using the considerable power and influence of the Convention to shape national political agendas in ways that earlier Baptists would have considered violations of the separation ideal. In so doing, the SBC is edging ever closer to the extreme theocratic views of what has been called Dominion Theology and the Reconstruction Movement, both of which are blatant expressions of "raw majoritarianism" and winner-take-all.

The Christian Reconstruction movement was launched in 1973 when a Presbyterian Minister, Rousas Rushdooney, published *Institutes of Biblical Law*, a 800-page 3-volume book on the application of the Ten Commandments to modern society. Rushdooney and his co-leader and son-in-law, Gary North, believe God's covenant with Adam required him to exercise dominion over the earth and to subdue it under God according to God's law. Rushdooney invites his followers to subdue all things and all nations to Christ and His law. His basic thesis is this: The only true order is founded on biblical Law, and Christians alone are biblically mandated to occupy all secular institutions until Christ returns. In his book, *Dominion Theology: Blessing or Curse,* Thomas Ice quotes the following passage from George Grant, a leading dominionist writer:

> Christians have an obligation, a mandate, a commission, a holy responsibility to reclaim the land for Jesus Christ—to have dominion in civil structures, just as in every other aspect of life and godliness. But it is dominion we are after. Not just a voice. It is dominion we are after. Not just influence. It is dominion we are after. Not just equal time. It is dominion we are after.
>
> World conquest. That's what Christ has commissioned us to accomplish. We must win the world with the power of the Gospel. And we must never settle for anything less. . . . Thus, Christian politics has as its primary intent the conquest of the land—of men, families, institutions, bureaucracies, courts, and governments for the Kingdom of Christ.[9]

The movement has a blunt distaste for pluralism and democracy. According to Frederick Clarkson, Gary North wrote in 1982 that in an effort to reach Baptists:

> We must use the doctrine of religious liberty. . .until we train up a generation of people who know that there is no religious neutrality, no neutral law, no neutral education, and no neutral civil

government. Then they will get busy constructing a Bible-based social, political and religious order which finally denies the religious liberty of the enemies of God.[10]

It is difficult to measure how deeply Dominion Theology and Reconstructionism have infiltrated the purposes of the new SBC leadership. Neither of these movements fit comfortably with the premillennial views held by most of the fundamentalists now in major positions of the Southern Baptist Convention, but some observers believe the influence of these winner-take-all philosophies runs deep. This is especially true since Paige Patterson and Paul Pressler, the two organizers of the SBC fundamentalist takeover, were interviewed by Reconstructionist Gary North in the famous "Firestorm Tapes" of 1986. They outlined their strategy for taking over the Southern Baptist Convention, which North boasted could be used to take over national institutions. According to Frederick Clarkson,

> The Reconstructionists have taken over the Southern Baptist Convention's national leadership. And they've made great inroads into denominations such as the Assemblies of God, which in the past have been radically apolitical. Southern Baptist spokesman John Revell (Editor of the SBC Executive Committee's journal, SBC Life) acknowledged that Reconstructionists and Baptists agree on many issues—from biblical infallibility to abortion to the primacy of men in the family and in church governance. But he denied the denomination is hell-bent on a dictatorship of the preachers. Revell said, "Christian Reconstruction would be, in practical terms, a theocracy. People who agree with that would be a small minority in his denomination. The church should not resort to assuming civil power."
>
> Revell is technically correct, but at the same time very wrong. Groups like the Southern Baptists won't use the word "theocracy." What they do support is religious majoritarianism. They push a religious political agenda they believe is best for everyone. And when the litmus test for political office is a list of religious issues, that's a problem for a society organized around religious pluralism. In the end, you end up with a society that is indistinguishable from the theocracy advocated by Reconstruction.[11]

Historically, because of frequent persecution by unfriendly majorities, Baptists have been staunch supporters of religious liberty, freedom of individual conscience, and separation of church and state. The Baptist ideal has always been that whatever group holds the majority in Baptist life, it's their responsibility to safeguard the rights of the minority—hear their concerns, value their input, respect their convictions, share opportunities and responsibilities with them as part of the Baptist family.

The Patterson/Pressler party complained that before the fundamentalist takeover, when majority leadership was in the hands of traditional Baptists, they were excluded. But while the record may not be perfect, there is clear evidence that before they gained control of the Convention, the fundamentalist and ultraconservative minority already had valid input in Convention organization and decisions. They were not arbitrarily excluded from the circle and were very much involved at every level of denominational life. They were simply not allowed to dominate or control.

The basic point is that in the work the Lord called us to do in the church, in a denomination of churches, or in the world, simple principles of Christlike behavior ought to prevail. There should be no hesitation to strive for higher-ground methods and procedures that lead to Christian civility. Avoiding raw majoritarianism in Christian organizations may be as simple as the Golden Rule, taking turns, sharing, fairness, compassion, and not ostracizing fellow believers. This is the least one could expect from followers of Jesus Christ.

With Liberty and Justice for All

One species of the Christian family might be called *Authenticus Baptistus*—Authentic Baptists. A number of important convictional genes distinguish this species from similar life forms in the family—convictions about God, Christ, salvation, the church, the Bible, and the ordinances. But there is one dominant gene in the species that stands out. It encapsulates many of the representative values of the species. That dominant convictional gene is freedom. Freedom lies deep in the DNA, the chromosomes of *Authenticus Baptistus*. We

Baptists are known by the genetic marker called freedom. Baptists historically have been in the front lines of the battle to preserve liberty and justice for all in our country.

When Paul was brought before the Roman authorities and they discovered that he was a Roman citizen, the chief captain boasted, "I bought my freedom for a large sum." Paul answered, "I was born free." (Acts 22:28)

Because of the freedom we have through faith in Christ, and because of the sacrifice of others to preserve it, Baptists too can say, "We were born free." Freedom is a part of our birthright, our life essence. True Baptists are free Baptists.

Baptists believe the Bible is the inspired word of God, and that every believer should have free access to the Bible. Each individual should have the freedom to interpret the Bible through independent reading as confirmed by the illumination of the Holy Spirit and understood within the community of believers. We should be free to preach and practice the truths of the Bible.

Of course, Baptists acknowledge that ultimate religious authority resides in our Lord Jesus Christ. He is the Living Word, whom we come to know through the Scriptures. It is under His lordship that Baptists claim the freedom to reject all manmade creeds and look to the Scriptures alone as our written authority for faith and practice.

When Southern Baptists organized their Convention in 1845, they planted that statement prominently in the founding documents. They made it clear that they intentionally refused to adopt any other creed than the Bible, referring to the historic Baptist aversion to manmade creeds.

Admittedly, the aimless uncertainty of our post-modern culture worries us. The bland absence of conviction nudges us to adopt creeds. Martin Marty describes the motifs of this culture as disorientation, marginality, fluidity, and a hodge-podge pluralism. Living in that kind of world tempts even Baptists to draw up firm statements of orthodoxy. But Authentic Baptists must resist that temptation and maintain our historic freedom from manmade creeds. While giving ample attention to careful theological reflection and formulation, we affirm our unashamed allegiance to the authority of Scripture and the freedom to claim Holy Scripture alone as our only creed.

We also affirm our freedom to search the Scriptures for ourselves. W. B. Johnson, first president of the SBC, called it the freedom "of each individual to judge for himself in his views of truth as taught in the scriptures."

Authentic Baptists identify with the Berean Christians in Acts 17:11. Even when Paul and Silas preached to them, they felt compelled to examine the Scriptures for themselves "to see if these things were so." Each Baptist is free to interpret biblical truth according to the personal dictates of individual conscience.

That's why true Baptists shudder when any majority group—including the present majority leadership of the Southern Baptist Convention—attempts to enforce on others not only our regular confessions of faith, but their own list of narrow beliefs about such things as women in ministry, eschatology, Calvinism, worship styles, and strict inerrancy.

In the past, remembering the biblical mandate "We ought to obey God rather than man," Baptists have literally died to preserve freedom from forced beliefs, and once again today, at the beginning of a new millennium, history cries out for courageous denominational patriots who will take up the cause of Bible freedom.

We need Baptist freedom fighters, modern-day Jeremiahs, who are unpurchasable, unshaken by the slander of our enemies, who refuse compromise, who are willing to sacrifice to preserve Bible freedom. We need courageous leaders who reject raw majoritarianism and are secure enough to allow dissent and fair-minded enough to respect and protect the minority. That's the Baptist way. That's the higher-ground way. That's Christian civility, and it needs to be lived out again before a world hungry to see it.

Conclusion

All three of the Synoptic Gospels record the incident near the close of Jesus' ministry when James and John (and their mother, according to Matthew) asked for special favors from Jesus. Specifically, they wanted to sit on His right and left hand in the kingdom. The other disciples were "indignant" at the two brothers, but Jesus called them to Him and said,

> You know that the rulers of the Gentiles lord it over them, and their great men exercise authority over them. It shall not be so among you; but whoever would be first among you must be your slave; even as the Son of Man came not to be served but to serve and to give His life as a ransom for many. (Matt 20:20-28)

It would seem elementary and indisputable that Christians should exhibit this spirit in their relationships with fellow believers. If the secular democracy we value in our country was careful in its founding documents to protect the minority from the "tyranny of the majority," if our founding fathers saw the need for safeguards to preserve simple fairness that would shield the welfare and the interests of the minority, if our Constitution exists in part to ensure a spirit of congenial consensus among fellow citizens who disagree, then surely, Christians—in particular our Baptist Christians—should go the second mile in our conventions and local churches to reject raw majoritarianism and give special attention to the minority—playing fair, taking turns, encourage everyone to participate, building consensus, treating others as they would want to be treated.

We have the clear command of the Lord Jesus. Not to obey Him is a sin.

Notes

[1] Ann Rodgers, "Campaigning for Civility and Compassion," *Christian Century* (2 November 2004), <http://www.findarticles.com/p/articles/mi_m1058/is_22_121/ai_n9507705>

[2] Robert H. Frank and Philip J. Cook, *The Winner-take-all Society* (New York: Penguin Books, 1995). From back cover of book.

[3] Ibid.,#4.

[4] "Democracy," Wikipedia Encyclopedia, <http://en.wikipedia.org/wiki/Democracy>.

[5] In a representative democracy, the majority is actually only a relative majority—a majority only of the voters who voted and is therefore actually a minority. For example, when followers of the fundamentalist takeover voted in a Southern Baptist

Convention meeting and won by fifty-one percent, they were indeed the majority of those voting in the meeting. In the largest of these conventions, that would be 20,000 people. But those 20,000 were a tiny minority of the 12,000,000 Southern Baptists they represented. It could be argued, therefore, that any tyranny is actually one minority "tyrannizing" another minority!

[6] Lani Guinier, *The Tyranny of the Majority: Fundamental Fairness in Representative Democracy* (New York: Simon & Schuster, 1995) 4.

[7] John D. Pierce, "Cooperation, Conversation Should Not Be Equated with Compromise," *Baptists Today* (February 2005): 7.

[8] Greg Warner, "IMB trustees tried power of press to silence dissent, Burleson says," Associated Baptist press release, 17 January 2006.

[9] George Grant quoted in Thomas Ice, *Dominion Theology: Blessing or Curse* (Portland: Multnomah Press, 1988) 412.

[10] Gary North, quoted in Frederick Clarkson, *Eternal Hostility: The Struggle Between Theocracy and Democracy* (Monroe: Common Courage Press, 1997), quoted by John F. Sugg, "America the Theocracy," *The Weekly Planet,* 25-31 March 2004, <http://www.weeklyplanet.com/2004-03-25/cover.html>.

[11] Ibid.

Moderation,
Not Extremism

Even though it's true, it's stating the obvious to say that the loss of civility in our national political discussions and in our denominational disagreements is largely the result of extremism. Sometimes there are "ultra" voices on both sides of a debate, but based on my personal observations, destructive extremism is usually introduced into an argument by hyperconservative fundamentalism. And the strident, angry confrontations and shrill, accusative tone of their public discourse thwarts any possibility of constructive and reasoned solutions.

In his recent book, former U.S. president Jimmy Carter addresses extremism in national political wrangling. He argues that the deterioration in harmony, cooperation, and collegiality in the Congress is, at least in part, a result of the rise of fundamentalism with its spirit of rigidity, domination, and exclusion. My experience with denominational extremism is similar. The caustic polarization in our Southern Baptist family was introduced by that identical fundamentalist spirit of "rigidity, domination, and exclusion."[1]

One way to reverse this growing incivility is to encourage the higher ground of moderation in our discourse and personal relationships. Now I admit that even though they're the linguistic opposites of "extremism" and "extremist," "moderation" and "moderate" are not the most appealing terms to use. Sometimes, the word "moderate" takes on unflattering connotations such as bland, average, so-so, soft, cheap, dispassionate, or sedated. It often carries the idea of someone without convictions, a wishy-washy who's afraid to take a stand.

I've never felt comfortable being labeled a "moderate" (any more than I suppose some ultraconservatives feel comfortable being labeled "fundamentalist"). One time I emphasized this discomfort by claim-ing, "I'm not a moderate. I don't even believe in moderate drinking!" Then I realized that could be taken two different ways! But modera-tion as the opposite of extremism is in most cases a noble and desirable position.

Dallas News columnist Steve Blow made this point in 1995 in his column promoting moderation.[2] He admitted it was not a popular position in a day when everybody is urged to "join the revolution, take no prisoners, go to the mat, feel the burn, hit the wall, search and destroy." He acknowledged the jokes about people in the middle of the road who get hit by traffic going in both directions. (I remem-bered a similar story of the Civil War soldier who decided on neutrality and wore a uniform with a gray jacket and blue trousers— only to be shot in the shoulder and the leg.)

I found myself siding with Steve Blow's approach, because I too have been cursed with the ability to see both sides of arguments. (Steve admitted his tombstone ought to read "But on the other hand. . . .") I also find it hard (like he does) to understand how extremists can boldly proclaim their arguments without acknowledging there might be other positions worth considering. He quoted a friend who said, "I wish I could be as sure about *anything* as that guy is about everything."

But moderation is not necessarily synonymous with lukewarm moral weakness. The word "moderate" and its noun form "modera-tion" actually convey something admirable when applied to civility in public discourse. The classic meaning of moderation is a position that avoids excesses and extremes; that is, temperate, restrained, prudent, fair, and reasonable. A moderate believes that the truth usually lies in the "golden mean" between extremes. Moderates aim for judicious tol-erance, a calm willingness to listen to and consider the convictions of those with whom they disagree. Without surrendering convictions, moderation seeks truth in the center, which is not always marked by a cowardly "yellow stripe." The "radical middle," as Gordon Fee calls it, is not bland neutrality, but it's the path that avoids the dangerous ditches on either side of the road. It's a courageous position held by people some have called "flaming moderates."

When I drove Dr. J. I. Packer from the airport to the "Inerrancy Conference" we sponsored for Baptists in North Carolina in 1987, he reminded me that as a conservative theologian he often fought the battle against extremism on both the right and the left. He opposed shallow liberalism on the left, but he also opposed hard-line fundamentalist legalism on the right. No one could accuse Packer of being wishy-washy or shy on theological convictions.

So my plea for the higher ground of Christian civility calls for sharing our convictions with moderation, not extremism. It is a position espoused by one of my Baptist heroes, E. Y. Mullins, theologian, apologist, philosopher, and Southern Seminary president, who died in 1928. My doctoral dissertation examined the apologetic method of Mullins, and my admiration for him has grown during the recent struggles within the denomination we both served as seminary presidents. Among other qualities, Dr. Mullins was a moderate in the good sense. He believed that "the really safe leaders of thought are between the extremes."

The importance of E. Y. Mullins as a Baptist scholar was expressed by his colleague at Southern Seminary, Professor Harold W. Tribble, who called him "the greatest thinker produced by Southern Baptists up to this time."[3] At Mullins's funeral in 1928, George Truett assessed his influence as "distinctive beyond that of any other Baptist in the world in recent years."[4] W. O. Carver praised him as "the best known Baptist in the world. He was unsurpassed in influence for good by any man in his denomination."[5] More recently, Fisher Humphreys appraised Mullins as "a responsible, careful theologian; he read widely; he thought carefully; he was constructive; he spoke to the concerns of his time; he was not rationalistic, narrow, vague, or overly defensive; he was a great Baptist theologian."[6]

When I was first introduced to E. Y. Mullins's book, *Why Is Christianity True*, in my classes at Southwestern Seminary, I felt I'd met a "kindred spirit." It was Mullins's distinctive approach to apologetics that first appealed to me. Having reviewed the class reading lists of leading twentieth-century apologists, I was struck by the scarcity of Baptist authors and, with this one exception, the outright absence of

Southern Baptists. Mullins was a delightful discovery because he was a Southern Baptist; he was "one of us"—he was even a Texas Aggie!

I liked him also because his localized identity as a Southern Baptist didn't make him parochial or provincial. He was a cosmopolite, a world Baptist. To Mullins, "Baptist" was not just another denominational brand name—no more than Handel is a musical brand name. "Baptist" stood for distinctives that Mullins treasured.

But his denominational commitment did not minimize his appreciation for other Christian groups or prohibit scholars of other denominational persuasions from benefiting from his writings. Princeton Seminary's J. Gresham Machen captured this cosmopolitan quality in his appraisal of Mullins:

> He has come to be spokesman not merely for the Southern Baptist Church (*sic*) or for the Baptist churches of America, but also to a considerable extent for the Baptist churches throughout the world. And there are many in other communions also who look to him as to their spiritual guide.[7]

A Centrist Between the Extremes

Among all his appealing qualities, the most engaging, it seems to me, was Mullins's ability to hold unreconciled doctrinal precepts in dynamic tension. On contradictory issues in theology, he usually stood between extremes. Mullins's approach was typically mediating and balanced, usually finding his position on the theological spectrum in "the radical middle." As Mullins expressed it, "The really safe leaders of thought, however, are between the extremes."[8]

This does not mean that the appropriate target for a doctrinal position is "dead center" between polarities. In fact, Mullins at times leaned toward the right and at other times toward the left. But by recognizing the importance of nuances and keeping antithetical ideas in tension, he carefully avoided the false extremes in the ditches on either side.

Some mistakenly believe this theological middle ground is a compromising position held by those who are reluctant to "take a stand."

For example, fundamentalist Al Mohler, in what appears to be either a misreading of Mullins or an unfortunate distortion of his theology, blames Mullins for "setting the stage for doctrinal ambiguity and theological minimalism."[9] Such categorization of E. Y. Mullins's balanced theological perspective as liberal exhibits a lack of appreciation of nuances in complex ideas and an unwillingness to live with the mystery of biblical paradox. This drive for "either-or" absolutism is counterproductive to constructive theological formation.

The following examples show how Mullins applied his centrist, moderating perspective to selected doctrinal issues.

Dynamic Tension Between Personal Experience and Biblical Authority

Because he emphasized Christian experience as a source of theological insight, Mullins's view has been criticized as a subjective substitute for the objective authority of Scripture. Mullins made it clear, however, that Christian experience is always under the authority of Christ as revealed in the Bible. When pushed to choose between the two, he always placed emphasis on the authority of the Bible.

Mullins claimed that the Bible is "the final authority in religion" and that Christ is "the final seat of authority in religion." The Bible and Christ should not be separated, but they are different. The Bible is literature and not the personal Christ, but the Bible is the only source for "the thoughts and truths and description of the life adjustments required to give us the vision of God in the face of Jesus Christ."[10]

Mullins centered authority in the will of God, which is embodied in Jesus Christ who therefore is the absolute religious authority. The authority of Jesus is expressed historically and objectively in the Scriptures, so that the Bible also is identified as our authority. "For Baptists, there is one authoritative source of religious truth and knowledge. It is to that source they look in all matters relating to doctrine, to policy, to the ordinances, to worship, and to Christian living. That source is the Bible."[11]

But we are not saved by belief in the Scriptures. We are saved by a living faith in Christ. For Mullins, Christ is the seat of authority in religion and is above and underneath and before the Bible. But the Bible is the authoritative literature that leads us to Christ.[12]

Dynamic Tension Between Individualism and Community

Among four characteristics of reliable Christian theology, James Leo Garrett points to the importance of the church in the work of theology. "It is the church, and not merely individual Christians, that is involved in the theological task."[13] Mullins would agree.

While at times he has been criticized for an undue emphasis on individualism in his theological method, it seems clear he understood that individual Christian experience does not function in isolation; it implies relationship and not mere solitude. Individual believers are not complete apart from the social relationship within which they function. Direct access to God under the concept of the priesthood of the believer and solidarity with the community of faith are complementary rather than mutually exclusive ideas.

If a man is incomplete apart from God, so is he incomplete apart from his brother. The interdependence and solidarity of the parts of the social organisms are commonplaces of sociological teaching. All human experience becomes socialized.[14]

Furthermore, the experience of the individual believer has to be consistent with the testimony of Scripture and the collective experience of the Christian community.[15] In his list of sources of religious knowledge, Mullins named Christ, Holy Spirit, Scriptures, and the experience of the redeemed—by which he meant *all* the redeemed in the historical community of believers.[16]

Dynamic Tension Between Sovereignty and Free Will

Mullins modified the high Calvinism of his predecessor, James Boyce, by balancing the extremes of Calvinism and Arminianism.

> Arminianism overlooked certain essential truths about God in its strong championship of human freedom. As against it, Calvinism ran to extremes in some of its conclusions in its very earnest desire

to safeguard the truth of God's sovereignty. We are learning to discard both names and to adhere more closely to the Scriptures, while retaining the truth in both systems.[17]

God's omniscience means that God knows everything that will occur, but this absolute foreknowledge does not predetermine an event's inevitability. "God's general plan included (man's) free choice."[18]

By adopting Kuyper's view that true Calvinism is a developing "life system" rather than a closed speculative system, Mullins was able to hold together both convictions—God's sovereignty and human freedom. Even though they seem contradictory, we must accept the fact that both ideas—human free will and non-coercive election—are affirmed by Christian experience. "Can we reconcile the sovereignty of God and human freedom in his electing grace? The answer is in the negative."[19] Mullins explained, "We are conscious of freedom as an ultimate fact of experience. We are driven to God's sovereignty as an ultimate necessity of thought."[20] But God's sovereignty is not that of an absolute, arbitrary Oriental monarch, but of a wise and loving Heavenly Father.

Dynamic Tension Between Millennial Theories

In discussing eschatology, Mullins took his trademark moderating position by emphasizing the basic elements about which most believers have agreed. Fisher Humphreys summarizes Mullins's view as follows:

> Following the death of the body, Christians enter a temporary intermediate state—not to be confused with purgatory or soul-sleep—to await their resurrection and the final judgment, when they will enter heaven and receive their rewards. The end of history will occur when Christ returns personally to the earth.[21]

It was Mullins's contention that the millennium had been given too much prominence in Baptist theology. For him, none of the millennial views was fully satisfactory. What really matters is the personal return of Christ, the resurrection of the body, and heaven and hell. Mullins distinguished clearly the biblical view of bodily resurrection from the Greek notion of the innate immortality of the soul.

Dynamic Tension Between Fundamentalism and Liberalism

The issues being debated at the time Mullins assumed leadership in the Southern Baptist Convention sound remarkably familiar. Debates focused on such things as Baptist origins (Whitsitt controversy), faith and science (evolution controversy), biblical authority, creedalism, inspiration, and infallibility. There were also accusations of liberalism in the seminaries, political conspiracies to control Convention agencies by electing single-minded trustees, confrontations of fundamentalists and moderate conservatives, threats to withhold funds from the agencies, and conflicts over church-state issues, the social gospel, and ecumenism.

Because the issues he faced are so similar to those confronting Baptists and other Evangelicals today, Mullins's scholarly, conservative, centrist method of dealing with them provides a timely model for contemporary denominational leadership. He rejected liberalism on the left with its disavowal of supernaturalism, but he also rejected fundamentalism on the right with its scholastic reliance on reason.

While he stood strongly for the fundamental doctrines of orthodox biblical theology and was enlisted to write one of the "Fundamentalist" tracts, he refused to be pigeon-holed or arbitrarily labeled by any theological faction. He was well aware of the dangers of both extremes, but in spite of the ferment and controversy of his era, he refused to panic or be stampeded into overreacting.

On the one hand, there could be no doubt about E. Y. Mullins's strong opposition to theological liberalism. In his inaugural address, Mullins graphically described the liberalism that prevailed in some sections of the theological world of his day: "The coat of arms of the present age is an interrogation point rampant above the prostrate forms of three bishops, or doubt exultant over dogma."[22] Concerned that such liberalism could dilute the biblical faith of Southern

Baptists, Mullins in 1915 summarized and opposed what he called "the tenets of liberal theology":

1. Biblical miracles are interpreted to bring them within the range of natural law or else are dismissed as unhistorical.
2. The narratives of the virgin birth, resurrection, and other miracles were produced by "literary inventiveness."
3. The Bible writers were no more inspired than other literary composers.
4. Religion cannot be derived from external authority; it must answer to the highest intellectual demands of the age.
5. The personality of Christ belongs wholly in the natural sphere; he was unique only in his superior spiritual life.
6. The preexistent Christ of Paul and John are products of primitive interpretation.
7. The resurrection was due to psychic experiences or visions and is not based on objective fact. So also the other miracles are to be explained in terms of religious psychology.
8. Jesus did not set himself forth as an object of worship; only a religious example.[23]

The president of Southern Seminary also spoke out intelligently against the negative influences of naturalistic evolution, rationalistic higher criticism, and the unbiblical tenets of Rauschenbusch's social gospel. He believed such liberal inroads called for a scholarly restatement of biblical authority.

But on the other hand, Mullins strongly disapproved of the legalistic, rationalistic position of the fundamentalists, which he also saw as a serious threat to Southern Baptist theology. He objected when fundamentalists from the seminary board set up what came to be called a "smelling committee" to periodically visit faculty members in their search for heresy.[24] During Convention debates, he openly worked toward the "defeat of Radicals and Extremists...who want to put the thumb screws on everybody who does not agree in every detail with their statements of doctrine."[25] He described the fundamentalists as "hyper-orthodox," "ultra-brethren," "lacking in common sense," and on another occasion, "big 'F' fundamentalists who agitated for control of the Convention and sought to 'harass and muzzle teachers in our schools.'"[26] Rebuking J. Frank Norris, the quintessential Baptist extremist, Mullins wrote,

> Some of you brethren who train with the radical fundamentalists are going over on Catholic ground and leaving the Baptist position. . . . A man who tries to pin his brethren down to stereotyped state- ments, such as your letter contains, has missed the Baptist spirit.[27]

In his ongoing conflict with fundamentalist leader T. T. Eaton, Mullins pointed out that he rejected both the "half Baptist" (or liberal) who never emphasized doctrinal belief and the "Baptist and a half" (or fundamentalist) who overreacted to doctrinal differences. (Eaton countered Mullins's challenge by saying he gloried in being a Baptist and a half!)[28]

As a constructive conservative, Mullins faulted both fundamental- ists and liberals for their extremism, which led to name-calling rather than fruitful communication. He warned of the destructiveness of bitter disputes. The divisiveness, the party spirit, the loss of trust, the diversion from the main functions of evangelism and missions are the inevitable results.

Mullins had little patience for what he called "abnormal doctrinal sensitiveness" that he encountered in certain of his brethren.

> I maintain that I have no right to refuse to call a Baptist my brother merely because he does not happen to be my twin brother, and I also maintain that another Baptist has no right to refuse to call me brother (and nag and torment me) because I am not his twin.[29]

Conclusion

In these factious, mean-spirited days of confrontational disputes, we can learn from the balanced, restrained, prudent, fair, and reasonable style of E. Y. Mullins. He demonstrated the importance of holding strong convictions, but sharing them with moderation, not extrem- ism. He's an admirable and persuasive example of the higher ground of Christian civility to which twenty-first-century believers ought to aspire.

Notes

[1] Jimmy Carter, *Our Endangered Values: America's Moral Crisis* (New York: Simon and Schuster, 2005) 5.

[2] Steve Blow, "A Modest Request for Moderation," *Dallas Morning News*, 17 May, 1995, C1.

[3] Harold W. Tribble, "Edgar Young Mullins," *Review and Expositor* 49 (April 1952): 125.

[4] George W. Truett, "Sermon Notes at Memorial Service for Mullins," unpublished handwritten notes in library of Southwestern Seminary.

[5] W. O. Carver, "Edgar Young Mullins—Leader and Builder," *Review and Expositor* (April 1929): 128.

[6] Fisher Humphreys, *Baptist Theologians* (Nashville: Broadman, 1990) 8.

[7] Russell Dilday, "The Apologetic Method of E. Y. Mullins," Ph.D. diss., Southwestern Baptist Theological Seminary, 1960, 183.

[8] E. Y. Mullins, *The Axioms of Religion* (Philadelphia: Judson Press, 1901) 8.

[9] Mohler's comments are quoted from a Southern Baptist Seminary press release written by James A. Smith, Jr., and posted by *Baptist Press.*

[10] Mullins, *Freedom and Authority*, 394.

[11] E. Y. Mullins, *Baptists and the Bible* (Nashville: The Sunday School Board of the SBC, n.d.), 3, cited in Dilday, 67.

[12] Mullins, *Freedom and Authority*, 393.

[13] James Leo Garrett, Jr., *Systematic Theology: Biblical, Historical, and Evangelical* (Grand Rapids: William B. Eerdmans, 1990) 5.

[14] Mullins, *Freedom and Authority*, 40.

[15] See for example his statement in his unpublished "Outline of Lectures," pp.55-56: "The individual consciousness is not final. It is the collective consciousness which brings the true deliverance as to experience."

[16] It has been pointed out that Mullins had little to say about the doctrine of the church in his systemic theology. The reason for this, Fisher Humphreys suggests, may be that the curriculum at the seminary during Mullins's time dealt with ecclesiology in the practical courses in pastoral ministry, not in systematic theology, which was Mullins's discipline. (Humphreys, *Baptists Theologians*, 334)

[17] Ibid., vii.

[18] Mullins, *Axioms*, 226-27.

[19] Mullins, *Christian Religion*, 347.

[20] Ibid., 348.

[21] Humphreys, *Baptist Theologians*, 343.

[22] E. Y. Mullins, "The Inaugural Address of E. Y. Mullins," *The Baptist Argus* (n.d.): 8, cited in Dilday, 15.

[23] E. Y. Mullins, "The Jesus of Liberal Theology," *Review and Expositor*, 12 (1915): 175.

[24] William E. Ellis, *A Man of Books and A Man of the People: E. Y. Mullins and the Crisis of Moderate Southern Baptist Leadership* (Macon: Mercer University Press, 1985) 54.

[25] E. Y. Mullins, "Letter to Livingston Johnson," 3 July 1925, unpublished, Pamphlet File, Southern Baptist Theological Seminary, Louisville KY.

[26] E. Y. Mullins, "Letters to George C. McDaniel," 25 July 1925, 30 April 1926, unpublished, Pamphlet File, Southern Baptist Theological Seminary, Louisville KY.

[27] E. Y. Mullins, "Letter to J. Frank Norris," 16 April 1926, unpublished, Pamphlet File, Southern Baptist Theological Seminary, Louisville KY.

[28] E. Y. Mullins, "Inaugural Address," 8.

[29] Mullins, "Baptist Higher Education in Kentucky," 1906, Pamphlet File, Southern Baptist Theological Seminary, Louisville KY, 18.

Constructive Conservatism, Not Carnal Conservatism

One evidence of the coarsening tone of public discourse in our country today is the widespread practice of categorizing or branding people on the basis of their supposed theological or philosophical positions. It's become a favorite tactic in the midst of an angry debate—especially if your argument is weak—to degrade opponents by consigning them to some unflattering classification. And the lexicon of labels available today provides endless choices.

Throughout his book *The Story of Christian Theology*, Roger Olson referred to a number of these labels used in the wider world of Christian theology. Some are not offensive, but others would probably not be received well by those being categorized. Here are a few he mentioned: "militant conservatives," "maximal conservatives," "progressives," "moderate-liberals," "neo-orthodox," "new modernists," "mainstream Protestants," "Protestant orthodox," "hyperconservatives," "Evangelicals," "early fundamentalists," "neoconservatives," "self-identified fundamentalists," "moderate-fundamentalists," "pietists," "conservative Evangelicals," "new Evangelicals," "Puritan-Princeton Evangelicals," "Pietist-Pentecostal Evangelicals," "progressive Evangelicals," "process thinkers," "liberationists," "eschatological thinkers." Olson concluded his excellent tome by acknowledging that the diversity of contemporary theological emphases can become a hopeless cacophony. But, with a glimmer of hope, he lifted up the possibility that "Diverse voices, when brought together in harmony, can make a chorus out of cacophony and a choir out of confusion."[1]

The recent controversies among Southern Baptists have produced a vocabulary of brand names unique to our own denominational diversity: "ultra-liberal," "liberal," "moderate-liberal," "hyperconservative," "hyper-orthodox," "maximal-conservative," "fundamentalist," "fundamental-conservative," "moderate," "moderate-conservative," even "ultra-moderate," *ad infinitum, ad nauseam*. All of these terms are imprecise and can be easily stretched, misused, and abused.

There's a story about a west Texas rancher who bought ten ranches and put them all together into one huge spread. When asked what he called his new ranch, the proud owner replied, "I just linked all ten names together and call it the "BarX, DoubleD, RockingR, LazyS, Frying Pan, CircleP, XIT, OK, TripleA, DiamondK Ranch." "Wow!" responded the impressed questioner. "You must have a lot of cattle!" "Well, actually, no," replied the rancher. "Not many of them survive the branding!" And civil discourse among Christians may not survive the branding either.

One problem with branding is the lack of agreement on what the brands signify. For example, the labels "conservative" and "liberal" among Baptists in the South are measured by one standard, but in most of the mainline denominations those same words are understood by a different standard. During my two-year term as president of the Association of Theological Schools in North America, representatives from seminaries related to Episcopal, Methodist, Presbyterian, and other mainline church groups couldn't help but laugh when they heard about accusations of liberalism in the Southern Baptist Convention. They joked that our worst Baptist "liberals" would probably seem closer to what they called "red-necked fundamentalists" in their denominations!

Classical theological liberalism, as popularly understood, would include denying the deity of Jesus, dismissing the Bible's inspiration and authority, rejecting anything supernatural, and a host of social and political positions that most orthodox believers would call heretical. In all my fifty-four years in church ministry and academia, I never encountered anything in Southern Baptist circles close to that kind of classical liberalism. Sure, we had a few professors, particularly among university faculties, who leaned more to the left than the average Southern Baptist would find acceptable, but even these would be considered "conservative" in the wider world of Christian thought.

Most of the colleagues who represented the 200 theological schools in the ATS—including mainline, evangelical, and Roman Catholic institutions—would categorize our Southern Baptist Convention as "conservative." Ironically, however, within our own SBC family, there were numbers of vocal fundamentalists who glibly branded fellow Baptists "liberals" simply because if they didn't agree with the stringent, hard-line standards of the takeover party.

At one point, would-be denominational peacemakers promoted the hybrid term "moderate-conservative" as a better word than "liberal" to distinguish traditional Baptists from fundamentalists. But that suggestion was quickly ridiculed by fundamentalists, who claimed it was an attempt to conceal their true liberalism. Speaking in a Convention pastor's conference, one of the hardliners ridiculed the term "moderate-conservative" by saying, "A skunk by any other name is still a skunk!" The loud applause that erupted in response to his comments indicated that in their eyes, "moderate-conservatives" were merely "liberals" with a new name.

The chair of the Southwestern Seminary Trustees, who had been placed on the board by the ultraconservative party that took over the SBC, reluctantly acknowledged in one of the meetings that our recent faculty appointments were theological conservatives. "But," he quickly added, "they are not *political* conservatives.'" That meant, he explained, that they refused to take up the banner of the Paige Patterson/Paul Pressler political party! Patterson himself on several occasions made a similar distinction, showing that sometimes these labels were arbitrarily applied not so much on the basis of theological conviction as on denominational party affiliation.

Actually, such labeling is nonsensical and shouldn't have been necessary. To be identified as "Christians" or even "Baptist Christians" should have been sufficient, but we learned that if we failed to initiate our own identifying category, then our antagonists, or at times the media, would do the labeling for us. As a result of this unfortunate pressure to categorize positions, Baptists in the South began to identify themselves by a plethora of labels, each claiming in one way or another to be "conservative." "Moderate-conservative," "fundamental-conservative," "compassionate-conservative," "political-conservative," "courageous-conservative," "Calvinist-conservative," and "Arminian-conservative." And even these titles often had nuanced subcategories.

In a lecture at Baylor University, David Solomon, a Baptist from Texas who teaches at the Center for Ethics and Culture at Notre Dame, said he had some friends who are "not liberal but a smidgeon more than moderate." Some of us have never been too fond of the term "moderate," so I guess you could say that Baptists like some of us are not fundamentalist but a smidgeon less than moderate.

The late John Newport, my PhD major professor and the provost and academic vice president at Southwestern during my time there, worked hard to help us find a term to describe our position. We wanted to show that a person could be conservative without being cranky, but the simple label "conservative" had been co-opted by the fundamentalists and, without modification, carried negative connotations. He proposed the term "constructive-conservative," and a number of "moderate-conservatives" who didn't especially like the designation "moderate" began to use it too.

Constructive-conservatives understand that theological nit-picking over minor issues is not productive, and that Christians should not waste their energies putting down other believers with whom they disagreed on inconsequential issues.

That's what Millard Erickson, then at Bethel Seminary, warned us about when he spoke at the 1990 Day-Higginbotham lectures at Southwestern Seminary. He said that we must not become ecclesiastical highway patrolmen spending our time setting radar traps to catch our brothers and sisters in what we consider to be violations and writing them theological citations.

So we made every effort to clarify the controversial issues and to enlighten the seminary's critics about our enthusiastic commitment to biblical truths and authentic Baptist ideals, but the fundamentalist criticism was based on emotion, not reason, and the labeling continued.

To add to the labeling mix, the recent book *Power Religion*, a corrective to evangelical abuses, introduced the term "carnal conservative."

Power Religion: The Selling Out of the Evangelical Church was published by Moody Press in 1992 and edited by Michael Scott Horton. It includes contributions by such evangelical luminaries as Charles Colson, D. A. Carson, James Boice, R. C. Sproul, Alister McGrath, and J. I. Packer. In the book, these "new Evangelicals" called for a reshaping of the conservative movement in order to correct certain evangelical abuses. They rejected and offered better alternatives to such excesses as: triumphalistic church growth strategies and authoritarian styles of pastoral leadership.[2]

The authors argued that such excesses have created a distorted Evangelicalism that Packer and others named "carnal conservatism." It's an unbiblical and dangerous breed of Evangelicalism, and they called for correctives that would lead to renewal.

In 1992, when *Power Religion* was published, Southwestern Seminary was experiencing the peak intensity of the fundamentalist assault with its unjustified accusations of "liberalism" and its board of trustees being stacked with hyperconservatives by the Patterson/Pressler political controllers. As president, I tried to use the popularity of the book to remind our constituents that there were different kinds of "conservatism." It was my contention that through the years, Southwestern had aimed at the informed and balanced position of "constructive conservatism," not "carnal conservatism." Echoing a popular country-western song, Southwestern was conservative when conservative wasn't cool! But our brand of conservatism avoided the legalistic and argumentative characteristics so often found in the militant fundamentalism of the Convention takeover party.

Carnal Conservatism

From the perspective of *Power Religion,* and from my own interaction with fundamentalism, what are the negative features of a flawed conservatism that justify its being called carnal? How does this variety of conservatism that rose to ascendancy in the Southern Baptist

Convention differ from the traditional conservatism that characterized the Convention in its previous century and a half?

I must begin by acknowledging my upbringing as a Southern Baptist. Since my father and mother spent lifetimes in Southern Baptist congregational and denominational ministry, I grew up totally immersed (excuse the pun) in that context. Most long-term Southern Baptists will understand the following markers of my experience: Vacation Bible Schools, Bible sword drills, Bible story-telling contests, summer youth camps, youth fellowships, youth choirs, Sunday School classes, Training Unions, Royal Ambassadors, missions, revivals, conventions, retreats at Glorieta, NM, and Ridgecrest, NC, and, of course, dinners on the ground. As my Baptist generation is used to saying, "I was Baptist born and Baptist bred, and when I die, I'll be Baptist dead!"

I admit some admiration for the ninety-year-old lifelong Baptist who was in the hospital, conscious, but without long to live. His family, who visited with him regularly, were surprised—no, shocked— to learn one day that he had called in the local Methodist minister and had joined the Methodist church. The family crowded into the hospital room demanding an explanation. "You've been a loyal Baptist all your life. Why would you join the Methodist church here at the end of your life?" "Well," he responded, "I figured since I was going to die soon, it would be better to lose one of them than one of us!"

So the following appraisal of "carnal conservatism" in our Southern Baptist life is shared from my experiential perspective as a "total immersion" Baptist.

The first feature of this flawed variety of Baptist conservatism has to do with what we lovingly call "Baptist distinctives." They're the commonly accepted convictions that have characterized traditional Baptists through the years. Of course, Baptists share with other Christian denominations core beliefs such as Trinitarian Christology, justification by faith, and other doctrines of evangelical orthodoxy. But Baptists have also held convictions, the combination of which might be called unique or distinctive. Here's a representative list:

- Regenerate church membership
- Believer's baptism by immersion
- No creed but the Bible
- Congregational church government and the autonomy of the local congregation
- Liberty of conscience, religious freedom, and separation of church and state
- Soul competency and the priesthood of each believer
- Symbolic ordinances of baptism and the Lord's Supper
- Security of the believer
- Voluntary cooperancy as the form of denominational structure

Unfortunately, these distinctives are threatened by serious attrition if not absolute extinction—not from outside attacks, but from "ultra-brethren" within the Baptist family. In their place, the fundamentalists now in charge of the Southern Baptist Convention have substituted alternatives:

- In the place of a democratic form of congregational government and a team approach to church ministry is a view of authoritarian pastoral leadership that borders on dictatorial. They claim the pastor "rules" the church.
- In the place of thoughtful discussions of doctrinal orthodoxy is the use of "shibboleths" such as the term "inerrancy" to determine acceptable beliefs. One fundamentalist detractor tried to get our faculty to use the term "inerrant" to describe their view of biblical authority. He said, "I know they hold to the absolute authority and trustworthiness of the Bible, and I know they have reservations about the term, but just get them to say, 'I believe the Bible is inerrant,' and the criticism will stop."
- In the place of separation of church and state is a less strict view that promotes mandated prayer in schools and other legislatively enforced morality. Some even propose the implementation of a "reconstructionist" form of theocracy.
- In the place of the priesthood of each believer is a forced uniformity to a set of pet doctrines prescribed by denominational autocrats. One spokesman for this brand of conservatism said, "The priesthood of the believer is a figment of some infidel's imagination."

- In the place of voluntary cooperancy is a top-down, hierarchical denominational structure that seeks to enforce conformity.
- In the place of mutual Christian submission is a view of male dominance and female subjection in marriage and in church leadership.
- In the place of diverse worship styles, this "carnal" form of conservatism insists on a single form as orthodox. One of the trustees at Southwestern gave his simplistic explanation: "If a church begins its worship service by singing *The Lord Is in His Holy Temple*, [which he considered formal, "high-church" music] that's a liberal church and it won't grow. But if they begin by singing *Because He Lives* [which he considered "evangelistic contemporary" music] that's a conservative church and it *will* grow."
- In the place of a simple Biblicism that considered the word of God to be the inspired and fully trustworthy authority for faith and practice is an insistence on an extreme variety of absolute inerrancy that most conservative Evangelicals reject in favor of what Millard Erickson calls "full inerrancy."[3]

Furthermore, a strict, five-point Calvinistic monergism is now emerging as another test of orthodoxy, along with a growing insistence on dispensational, pre-tribulation, pre-millennialism. Others demand a strict view of creation, claiming creation was completed in six twenty-four-hour days, and that it must be dated within the last ten- to four-thousand years.

This flawed variety of Baptist conservatism is creedalistic, rationalistic, absolutistic, and separatistic. Most of those in SBC leadership today insist on complete separation from those who disagree with them on doctrine, lifestyle, politics, and virtually everything else. But they go even farther. They practice what Roger Olson calls "secondary separation," that is, separating from other conservatives who don't separate from those they consider liberal.[4] More than a few of these carnal conservatives follow the philosophy that the ends justify the means, allowing them to excuse misrepresentations, threats, and other devious strategies.

The above list of flaws is certainly not exhaustive and is based on personal experience rather than research, but it sounds very similar to the descriptions of "carnal conservatism" in *Power Religion*:

- Authoritarian styles of pastoral leadership
- Use of secular political strategies
- Fanning of emotional fears by supposed conspiracy theories
- Government entanglement that tends to reduce the church to nothing more than another political special-interest group
- Use of peer pressure, ostracization, and withholding rewards to enforce conformity (ganging up)
- Total defeat of those who disagree (an ugly version of denominational ethnic cleansing)

Constructive Conservatism

What does constructive conservatism look like? Or a better question: "What would a new organization of Baptists in the South committed to constructive conservatism look like?" Now that the Southern Baptist Convention has been radically reshaped by fundamentalists who successfully won control by their inappropriate but effective political strategy, what will be the future shape of southern (lowercase "s") Baptists who no longer consider themselves Southern (uppercase "S") Baptists?

There have been several attempts to create alternative denominational options for disenfranchised Baptists in the South, only one of which, the Cooperative Baptist Fellowship, has survived and continues to grow in some parts of traditional Southern Baptist territory. Other Baptists have been able to find a denominational home in state conventions such as Virginia and Texas that have successfully resisted the fundamentalist effort to capture control as they did in the SBC. Some have linked up with other national Baptist bodies or have found international fellowship with the Baptist World Alliance.

In my opinion, the day of huge, bureaucratic, national, denominational organizations is over. Like the breakup of large corporations into smaller, more flexible, and profitable units (for example the telephone companies called "Baby Bells"), Baptist denominational life in the future will likely be more regional and smaller in scope. The emphasis will be on local congregations, area associations, and state conventions, and these will seek ways to form networks for efficiency and effectiveness in the place of lumbering and overgrown national conventions.

If a group of twenty-first-century Baptists in the South were to shun carnal conservatism and organize themselves into a denominational body committed to constructive conservatism, what would that body look like?

1. *Constructive conservative Baptists, as the term conservative implies, would preserve and treasure the best of the past as it takes on new forms in the future.* In *Habits of the Heart,* Robert Bellah wrote about the importance of places of memory, of keeping the old ways alive and visible as new forms are shaped. Similarly, I believe constructive conservatism will value the past, bringing forward and maintaining the best of our distinctive character, heritage, and identity, but in vigorous new forms, enlivened by the Holy Spirit.

2. *In a similar vein, a constructive conservative Baptist body would preserve denominational solidarity, but would be less afraid of responsible trans-denominational networks and coalitions.* Traditionally, Baptists have shied away from close associations with other denominations—even evangelical denominations to which we generally acknowledge some kinship. Now the time is right for Baptists to broaden the cooperancy that is so characteristic of our internal relationships and include in our cooperation a larger segment of like-minded believers in other groups, particularly in the evangelical world. Without diluting our distinctives or leaping carelessly into ecumenical alliances, we can find ways to work together and draw strength from our evangelical "cousins."

So constructive conservative Baptists, while jealously maintaining their denominational solidarity, would turn away from un-Christlike pride, smug exclusivism, and the unlovely triumphalism so prevalent among Baptists in the past.

3. *A constructive conservative Baptist body would refuse to use politics, power, and pressure tactics and adopt instead spiritual weapons such as persuasion and proclamation in its service for Christ.* In 1984 the SBC annual sermon, "Higher Ground," warned Southern Baptists to turn from "the muddy swamps of political coercion to the higher ground of spiritual persuasion." Jesus made it unmistakably clear by his commands and example that the power we're to employ in our work for Him is not political or conscriptive power, but spiritual power. Our Savior wept over Jerusalem, but He never besieged it, never rallied its legislature or courts to favor His cause, never formed a political coalition to advance His kingdom. He preached, prayed, served, loved, and, even at the sacrificial cost of His life, steadfastly rejected worldly force.

Baptists in the future need to imitate their Lord, who, even though He could wither a fig tree at fifty paces with a spoken rebuke and with one word de-fang a howling windstorm into a whimpering breeze, refused to force His will on others. Constructive conservative Baptists would adopt the biblical model and be content with spiritual weapons.

4. *A constructive conservative Baptist body would welcome and encourage believing intellectualism and reverent scholarship.* It would champion a scholarly, thoughtful, conservative, biblical theology that aggressively engages secular modernity without obscurantism, putting faith and reason in proper perspective.

The secular philosophy that dominates so much of society today may have grown not so much from a conspiracy of atheistic educators and political leaders as from the negligence of carnal conservatives who surrendered the scholarly turf to liberalism.

Unfortunately, some carnal conservatives are afraid of education and suspicious of intellectual reflection. This irrational fear was behind much of the criticism the seminaries received during the controversy. Remembering that Jesus commanded us to love God with "all our mind" (Matt 22:37), constructive conservative Baptists would counteract this widespread fear by a firm commitment to study and learning.

5. A constructive conservative Baptist body would be non-creedal, but at the same time it would be willing to articulate biblical doctrines with greater precision, taking more pains to think out convictions and to express them clearly. In contrast to the scholastic approach of other Evangelicals with their intricate doctrinal nuances and detailed qualifications. (e.g., the Chicago Statement on Inerrancy), Baptists historically have been "simple Biblicists." Constructive conservative Baptists would still maintain that uncomplicated view that the Bible is God's inspired word. They would continue their aversion to manmade creeds, their mistrust of fallen human reason, and their unashamed allegiance to the authority of Scripture. However, as constructive conservatives, they would give more attention to careful theological reflection and formulation.

6. A new constructive conservative Baptist body would seek a healthier balance between the personal and social implications of the gospel of Jesus Christ, improving on the steps we have already taken to coordinate evangelism and social ministry. The neo-evangelical model that emerged after World War II helped the old Evangelicalism realize that conservative theology with its call to aggressive evangelism does not exclude equally aggressive efforts to meet humanity's social needs.

Constructive conservative Baptists of tomorrow would understand that legitimate concerns for the eternal salvation of the lost need not conflict with, but should actually complement and inform, equally legitimate concerns for human suffering and injustice in the here and now.

7. A new constructive conservative Baptist body would continue to rely on "cooperancy" as the relational glue that holds it together in its primary task of obeying the great commission. It might be expressed in new organizational patterns, but cooperation would remain as the distinctive method of Baptist missions and education. There would be a willingness to include all like-minded Baptists in cooperative efforts to accomplish the overwhelming tasks our Lord has given us, realizing that within the boundaries of our common theological convictions, "Baptist diversity" is not only possible, but desirable.

Shaping a twenty-firstcentury body committed to constructive conservatism is a challenge worthy of the effort and support of every like-minded Baptist. Not only would such an effort strengthen Baptist churches in the future, but it would make a valuable contribution to the restoration of civility in denominational and public life. But such a new beginning may not come about merely by human effort

Who can forget the dramatic political changes that erupted in the former Soviet Union and Eastern Europe, bringing down Communism and walls of oppression that experts thought were immovable? These sudden transformations were not brought about by military assault or international negotiation, but by an irrepressible shared vision that spontaneously arose among thousands of individuals. In His omnipotent providence, God often surprises even the experts.

When we constructive conservative Baptists begin to dream again about new beginnings, when we start talking to each other about possibilities, and, more importantly, when we ask the Lord to bless our quest, a shared vision may emerge among our people. That's the Baptist way, and we can be sure that such a vision empowered by the Holy Spirit would be irrepressible and would eventually become a reality.

Perhaps the goal of actualizing a new body of constructive conservative Baptists can be achieved the same way—through a common vision so exciting in its possibilities that it challenges all of us to cooperate toward its ultimate fulfillment.

> For still the vision awaits its time. . . . If it seem slow, wait for it;
> it will surely come, it will not delay. (Habakkuk 2:3)

Notes

1 Roger E. Olson, *The Story of Christian Theology* (Downers Grove: InterVarsity Press, 1999) 609.

2 Michael Scott Horton, ed., *Power Religion: The Selling Out of the Evangelical Church?* (Chicago: Moody Press, 1992).

3 Millard J. Erickson, *Christian Theology*, v0ol. 1 (Grand Rapids: Baker Book House, 1983) 234.

4 Olson, *The Story*, 567.

Conclusion

That term "conclusion" suggests a wise, concise wrapping up of the primary theme of this book, which is a call for Christian civility. And that's what I'll try to do. Most of us have a built-in hunger to have complex issues simplified. We're like the lawyer who came to Jesus in Mark 10:28 asking him to sum up God's requirements in one simple obligation: "What is the first commandment of all? Boil it all down to one uncomplicated summary."

That must have been in the mind of "The Preacher" who wrote Ecclesiastes. He concludes in Ecclesiastes 12:13, "Here is the conclusion of the matter: Fear God and keep his commandments; for this is the whole duty of man. For God will bring every deed into judgment, with every secret thing, whether good or evil." That's simple, to the point, profound. In like manner, we expect the "conclusion" of a book or an essay to give us the gist of the argument. (Maybe so we won't have to wade through the entire composition!)

The word "gist" comes from an old French and Middle English word meaning "an abode." It's also related to the Latin word "to recline" or "to lie down" and is used in law to describe "where the real meaning lies." The gist of an argument is its essence or main point.

(My professor, John Newport, was the last lecturer on a crowded program once, and the moderator, looking at his watch and realizing it was getting late, introduced him by asking if he might be able to "give us just the gist of your lecture." John answered, "But it's *all* gist!")

Even though I believe my book is all gist, here is my effort to boil it down into a simple form. One solution to the rude coarsening of social interaction in our country and in our church life is the simple individual practice of Christian civility. After all, rudeness is a moral and spiritual issue—even a Christian issue. Individual believers can help rescue our country and our denominations from incivility by passing kindness forward, by the simple but powerful acts of Christian grace described in this book.

If that appears to be too difficult a task, then just take a baby step. Try pretending to be polite. Tackle just one of the qualities of Christlikeness until it becomes habitual. Then take up another one. Simply start acting on the basis of what Richard Mouw calls in the title of his book "uncommon decency." If enough Christians do it, their individual actions will impact the whole. Aristotle claimed that when individuals try to be good in small things, they are actually improving general morality. It's amazing what one or two people can do to influence society.

The Sigma Phi Epsilon fraternity house on the campus of the University of Washington had always been a typical "animal house" with boozy parties every Tuesday and Thursday, hazing violations, raucous nights, and dirty carpets. The house had become a repulsive pigsty. One former resident of the SigEps house said because the lights were always burned out, battered sofas were on the front porch, and the halls were so gross, he tried not to leave his room. There was the odor of stale beer, regular street brawls, and a reputation that kept coeds away and parents weeping when they dropped off their sons at the house.

But recently, a small group of fraternity brothers decided to clean up their act, and they instituted a Sigma Phi program called "Balanced Man." Most of the members left, but those who remained cleaned house—literally—not only scrubbing windows, bathrooms, and carpets, but shifting their reputation to emphasize a culture of civility.

New members are now recruited on the basis of academic performance, work habits, community service, and interest in good clean fun. They take etiquette classes, go to ballets, and not only are coeds no longer afraid to go near the place, but they even have parent's night once a month. Today they're one of UW's most successful fraternities academically. No wonder the fraternity's membership is rapidly growing. It all started with individual action.[1]

Lynne Truss, author of the popular book *Eats, Shoots & Leaves,* acknowledged that society tends to be suspicious of people who do good things for no reason—like feeding dimes into someone else's parking meter, but such actions in small things have an impact on the bigger picture. She believes these small contributions of civility make a person a genuine hero:

> In the absence of adequate street-lighting near my house, I do keep an outside light constantly burning in a spirit of general helpfulness, so maybe I am a modern saint after all. Phew. When they make lists of heroines in the future, this outside-light thing will doubtless ensure me a place alongside women who rowed lifeboats in tempests and tended the gangrenous in the Crimea. They can put it on my gravestone: "She lit the way for others." And underneath, "On the other hand, she was a shockingly bad recycler."[2]

To sum it all up then, twenty-first-century Christians can be heroes of civility. They can help our nation and our churches recover a civil quality of life that will infuse our attitudes and our actions, our thoughts and our work, our love and our pleasures. Christian civility is simply genuine Christian living! That kind of life comes from only one Source because, in the end, Christian civility, like the Christian life, is Christ.

One of our Sunday class members was waiting in line at the post office during this year's hectic Christmas season. The line moved slowly, those waiting became impatient, and one grouchy woman at the end of the line expressed her frustration loudly. She complained about the inept clerks, the bad parking, and the unprofessional management of the United States Postal Service. Looking at her watch, she let everybody know she was late to work, as though everybody else in line had nothing important to do. Everybody glared, and some mumbled, "Just cool it, lady. We're all in a hurry too." But one young woman who was standing quietly next in line to the window turned and said with genuine kindness, "Here. Trade places with me. You can have my place." Instant stunned silence gripped the lobby! With a chastened "thank you" from the grouch and admiring smiles from the others in line, the two women traded places.

Our Sunday school member concluded, "As a Christian, I wish I'd thought of that!"

Notes

[1] See article in *The Seattle Times*, 13 December 2005, and featured on NBC's *Today Show*, 15 December 2005.

[2] Lynn Truss, *Talk to the Hand* (New York: Gotham Books, 2005) 191.

On Higher Ground

Convention Sermon
Southern Baptist Convention
June 13, 1984
Russell H. Dilday

Introduction

The title of the message is taken from a well-known hymn:

> Lord, lift me up and let me stand,
> By faith on Heaven's tableland,
> A higher plane than I have found,
> Lord, plant my feet on higher ground.

The biblical text for the message is Philippians 3:14, "I press toward the goal for the prize of the upward call of God in Christ Jesus," and Colossians 3:1-2, "If then you were raised with Christ, seek those things which are above where Christ is, sitting at the right hand of God. Set your mind on things above, not on things on the earth."

The Bible repeatedly calls us upward to higher ground, to turn our backs on the petty, the trivial, and the unworthy, and to take instead the high road of uncompromising integrity. We are to stand on higher ground with the One who Himself is high and lifted up.

A video of Russell Dilday's sermon "Higher Ground" is
available at www.helwys.com

To every man there openeth A Way and Ways, and a Way,
The High Soul climbs the High Way, The Low Soul gropes the Low,
And, in between, on the misty flats, the rest drift to and fro,
And every man decideth, The Way his soul shall go.
(John Oxenham)

The challenge of the message to this Convention is that we obey the word of God that calls us to a more excellent way, and redeploy our messengers, our institutions, and our churches to God's tableland where they belong.

Our hearts have no desire to stay,
  Where doubts arise and fears dismay,
Though some may dwell where these abound,
  Our prayer, our aim is higher ground.

I. Let's turn from the misty flats of forced uniformity to the higher ground of autonomous individualism.

Baptists have stood tall in their courageous defense of individual autonomy. We call it "the priesthood of the believer," "the axiom of soul competency." It's that cherished truth that no one can stand between a person and God, except the one mediator, Jesus Christ. No church, no priest, no ordinance, no creed, nothing but Jesus. Our heroes have been those rugged individuals who died for the right to answer to God for themselves and to worship him as they pleased.

We take that concept of individualism from the Bible. Psalm 49:5 says, "None of them can by any means redeem his brother nor give to God a ransom for him." God created us individually, and each of us is both responsible and free to live his own life. That's why Jesus asked the disciples in Matthew 16:31 not only "Whom do men say that I am?" but "Whom do YOU say that I am?" And one of the clearest verses about individual autonomy is John 18:34, where Jesus confronted Pilate with the question, "Are you speaking for yourself, or did others tell you this?"

But unfortunately, in contradiction to the Bible, there are some among us who, fearful of standing alone, and determined to get ahead in denominational life, surrender that sacred privilege of individualism. They go along with the crowd, accepting the canned thinking of the majority. Swayed by public opinion, and glibly mouthing the popular clichés of the party in power, they are quick to espouse those causes that are in vogue. They cater to the powerful, play to the gallery, and flow with the tide, find some parade and begin to march in front of it.

Isn't it a shame to be caught in the grip of a mentality like that? Even if only one person among us believes that to get recommended to a better church you have to signal your loyalty to the party in power by using certain flag words. If you disagree, you'll be labeled. Be careful who you sit with in the sessions or talk to in the halls. Watch out how they see you vote. You may have a deep conviction about the issue being decided, but you'd better raise your ballot with the majority. Even if only one believes that, he is one too many. And over the dying ashes of autonomous individualism we will hear the probing question of Jesus: "Are you speaking for yourself, or did others tell you this?"

But lost individualism has another side. One side is the fear of standing alone, but the other side is the refusal to let another person stand alone. In his famous novel, George Orwell painted a grim picture of society in 1984, a society of forced uniformity. Everyone was obliged to mouth the party line or else. Spies listened and reported any diverse unorthodoxy to the Ministry of Truth. Individual disagreement was punished as heresy.

Incredible as it sounds, in 1984, there is emerging in this denomination, built on the principle of rugged individualism, an incipient Orwellian mentality. It threatens to drag us down from the high ground to the low lands of suspicion, rumor, criticism, innuendoes, and guilt by association and the rest of that demonic family of forced uniformity. I shudder when I see a coterie of the orthodox watching to catch a brother in a statement that sounds heretical, carelessly categorizing churches as liberal or fundamentalist, unconcerned about the adverse effect that criticism may have on God's work. But surely this would never happen in our Convention, would it?

Three experiences I've had recently lead me to say it might happen here. Last year, a pastor publicly critiqued the book I wrote on biblical authority. It was a broadside criticism in which he disagreed vehemently with my position. That's okay, except for the fact that he obviously misunderstood my position. Much of the criticism was so unjustified that it was obvious: he couldn't have read the book. I called him; he acknowledged that he wrote the criticism without having read the book for himself. I sent him a copy, and we eventually established an open relationship of discussion. But as I reflected on that experience, I couldn't help but remember the question of Jesus: "Are you speaking for yourself, or did others tell you this?"

Illustration number two: We had on campus recently a preacher who during our recent controversies has been very vocal in his defense of the denomination. He would be labeled by some as liberal or moderate. He preached a powerful biblical sermon in chapel that moved our student body and visiting guests. There were rousing "amens" and spontaneous ovations. After the service, one of our guests said to me, "I was really going to let you have it, Mr. President, for inviting that liberal to preach today, but I was wrong. That was a great message, but do you think he really believes what he preached today?" It was obvious the guest had let other people shape his opinion of our preacher, and I remembered the Scripture, "Are you speaking for yourself, or did others tell you this?"

Number three. A few years ago I attended one of those Bible conferences where criticism was so often leveled at our seminaries. The rhetoric was especially hostile that day. Later, upon discovering I was present, some of those who spoke so strongly came by to say, "I didn't have you in mind. I'm not really with this crowd; I'm for you." Well, the disclaimers may have been sincere, but I couldn't help but remember the biblical admonition in Colossians 3:22: "Serve the Lord with singleness of heart, not with eye service as men-pleasers," and the passage: "Are you speaking for yourself, or did others tell you this?

How much better to be a godly individualist who with open mind listens to all sides of an issue, prayerfully measures those issues by the word of God, and then humbly takes a position and stands courageously by it no matter what others think. How much better, like Luther, facing abuse if necessary, to say, "Here I stand. I cannot do otherwise, God help me." And how much better it is to allow that same freedom to others without pressing for lock-step uniformity. That's the rugged individualism to which the Bible calls us. And that's the higher ground where we Baptists have stood and where we need to stand today.

Let's turn from the misty flats of forced uniformity to the higher ground of autonomous individualism.

II. Let's turn from the muddy swamps of political coercion to the higher ground of spiritual persuasion.

Jesus made it unmistakably clear by his commands and example that the power we are to employ in our work for him is not political or conscriptive power, but spiritual power.

Consistently, Jesus refused to use even subtle coercion in his mission. He rejected the low ground of political force and chose instead the higher ground of spiritual persuasion.

Our Savior wept over Jerusalem, but He never besieged it, never rallied its legislature or courts to favor his cause, never formed a political coalition to advance his kingdom. He preached, and prayed, and served, and loved, and even to the point of sacrificial death, He steadfastly rejected worldly force. Jesus chose the higher ground of spiritual persuasion.

Heaven's entire angelic army was at his command. With the snap of a finger, He could have brought Herod and Pilate to their knees in surrender and enthroned himself King in Jerusalem. But He didn't. John 6:15 says, "Perceiving then that they were about to come and take Him by force to make Him king, Jesus withdrew again to the mountain by Himself." He came not to be an autocrat, but a servant leader.

John 9:54 says that even though James and John thought it was a great idea, Jesus would not call down fire from heaven on those who disagreed with him. Respecting that fragile jewel called free will, Jesus refused to manipulate, coerce, or commandeer the people. He chose persuasion, reason, and love as his weapons. He who could wither a fig tree at fifty paces with a spoken rebuke, and with one word de-fang a howling windstorm into a whimpering breeze, would not force his will on others. Jesus could have pulled the trigger of his power and with one divine laser blast vaporized the ones who nailed him to the cross, but instead He prayed, "Father, forgive them, for they know not what they do.

In Matthew 26:52 Simon Peter drew his weapon in the garden, and Jesus rebuked him. "Put your sword back into its place, for all who take up the sword will perish by the sword." We can learn from that verse, for it may seem appropriate at times for us to enlist the civil powers of the state in our witness for Christ. But beware, that's the low road to the misty swamps, not the way to God's higher ground.

Baptists have been best when we've used spiritual persuasion to get the work done—not political organization and coercion. We've been the people who, in the minority most of our history, have been content to use preaching, and witness, and prayer, not political alliances.

Go ahead. Engage the government as your ally. Since we're a major political force today, and hold the power to influence Congress, let's breech the wall of separation and bend the guarantees of religious liberty a little bit so that our faith enjoys the support of the state. It sounds like a good idea. If the sword of federal support is offered, grasp it. Use it. But watch out, Jesus said, "They that take up the sword will die by the sword."

Call on Big Brother in Washington to help you witness and worship, and Big Brother will trivialize your Lord, reducing His sacred birth to nothing more than a folk festival, giving Bethlehem's manger no more significance than Santa's sleigh or Rudolph's red nose. Ask the Supreme Court to endorse your Christian faith, and they will relegate the virgin-born Jesus, the only begotten of the Father, the King of kings and Lord of lords, they will relegate Him to the company of Frosty the Snowman and Alvin the Caroling Chipmunk.

Oh Baptists, it's better to have enemies who know who Christ is and detest him than political friends in high places who classify the eternal word of God with fairy tales.

Some day in the future, as so often in the past, other political forces hostile to religious liberty will hold the advantage. They will have the political clout you have today, and they may breech that crack you so casually made in the wall of separation, and circumvent the guarantees you brazenly bent a little bit, and they may steal away the liberty you carelessly abused. And future generations of Americans will look back on our twentieth century and wonder what happened to that country which a Baptist musician described as "sweet land of liberty."

Have you ever studied the sad experience of Baptists in Germany during Hitler's rise to power? We who've never lived under a repressive regime like the Third Reich should be slow to condemn, but the lessons of their failure are so timely. Church historian Stephen Brachlow has a disturbing study you ought to read.

German Baptists, rightly concerned about immorality in their country in the 1930s, rallied behind Hitler's drive to rid society of pornography, prostitution, homosexuality, and other social sins. Deceived by the Orwellian double-speak of Nazi propaganda, and impressed with Hitler's righteous campaign against degenerates and his pious commitment to what he called "positive Christianity," German Baptists temporarily lost sight of their traditional antipathy toward establishment religion. They developed alliances with the government and received unprecedented privileges while other religious groups were being persecuted. As one Baptist leader put it, "the German Finance Ministry favored Baptist churches in tax matters and the Secret Police were uninterruptedly friendly." For the first time in 100 years, German Baptists enjoyed the paternal care of their government. In contrast to their forebears who had struggled as a persecuted minority, they were now the privileged ones.

They dismissed the government restrictions placed on Lutheran and Evangelical congregations as divine judgment for the years they had harassed Baptist churches. So long as they remained unmolested by the authorities, these Baptists shrank from endangering their own privileged freedom by challenging the state. And they discovered too late that they were duped.

The lesson is clear. Individual Baptists should be involved as Christian citizens at every level of our democratic processes in government, but only to insure that personal freedom and justice are maintained, never to secure privileged support from the state nor encourage its entanglement in religious affairs. We must never give up our historic concern for religious liberty. Even when we find ourselves in positions of prominence and in league with the powerful, we must not fail to protect the freedom of the minorities who differ from us.

Oh twentieth century Baptists, where is your distinctive biblical message: "Render unto Caesar the things that are Caesar's and unto God the things that are God's"? Where is your voice, so consistently raised in past days, for religious liberty? Where is your ancient conviction that it is "not by might nor by power, but by God's spirit" that we conquer?

We should put away the sword of government alliance and political clout, and reclaim our historical Baptist legacy of separation of church and state. We must choose as Jesus did, to employ only spiritual weapons. Baptists don't have to look to a benevolent uncle in Washington. We have an omnipotent Father in heaven!

Let's turn from the muddy swamps of political coercion to the higher ground of spiritual persuasion.

III. Let's turn from the barren plains of egotistic self-interest to the higher ground of Christlike humility.

Who can forget that embarrassing incident in Mark 10:37 when James and John asked their special favor of Jesus? He had just predicted in graphic detail how He would soon be crucified, how they would mock Him, scourge Him, expose Him, and kill Him. And do you remember how James and John responded to that solemn prediction? They said to Jesus, "Grant us that we may sit, one on your right hand and the other on your left in your glory." Incredible! In fact, it seems Jesus was always catching the disciples at each other's throats

about who was the greatest. No wonder the Holy Spirit inspired Paul
to write in Philippians 2:3-7,

> Let nothing be done through selfish ambition or conceit,
> but in lowliness of mind let each esteem another better
> than himself. Let each of you look out not only for his
> own interest, but also for the interests of others. Let this
> mind be in you which was also in Christ Jesus,. . . who
> emptied Himself by taking the form of a servant..

The moment we imitate James and John in looking for personal
advancement, or the moment we imitate the Pharisees in seeking the
chief seats, in that moment we are bogged down in the barren plains
of egotistic self-interest. But the moment we imitate Jesus, let His lowliness of mind be our example, in that moment we climb to the higher
ground of Christlike humility.

Weren't you shocked to read that the U.S. government, following
the military rescue mission in Grenada, awarded 8,614 decorations for
bravery in action? We were shocked because only 7,000 troops were
involved in the fighting. Many of the medals for bravery under fire
went to bureaucrats in the Pentagon or Fort Bragg who sat behind
desks and were never in danger. We really know how to congratulate
ourselves, don't we? Somebody said God created us with our arms out
in front to make it almost impossible to pat ourselves on the back, but
we learned to do it anyway. We're experts at giving ourselves medals,
promoting our own careers, and looking out for number one.

I had a luncheon a while back for a famous television evangelist
who is often introduced as "the next Billy Graham." His secretary
called to ask if I would please arrange for a private room. She said the
evangelist was so well known that he could never eat at public restaurants. His fans would mob and interrupt his meal. Well, it sounded a
little presumptuous, but I followed her suggestion for privacy.

However, I couldn't help but remember my moment of glory a
few years ago in Atlanta when I entertained the *real* Billy Graham. The
crusade committee asked me to arrange a golf game and a luncheon
on Monday. I was really excited. The best golf courses were closed on

Mondays, so I pulled strings and enlisted the famous golf pro at the Atlanta Country Club to open his course just for Dr. Graham and our foursome. Then, I set up an elegant luncheon in one of Atlanta's best restaurants.

But when I called Dr. Graham to tell him my plans, do you know what *he* asked me to arrange? After hearing my suggestions, he thanked me, but humbly asked that we might make some changes. He would rather play at a public golf course and eat at a cafeteria near the hotel. I couldn't believe it.

When I picked him up, Dr. Graham had on an old golf cap and dark sunglasses, and we played on the sorriest golf courses in Atlanta, right under the flight path of the airport. Then, believe it or not, we pushed our trays through the line at Morrison's Cafeteria for lunch. There I was fighting an irresistible urge to point to this man in golf cap and sunglasses and say to everybody, "Do you know who this is? Do you know who I'm with?" No one recognized him until halfway through the meal, and he greeted that one nervous intruder graciously and kindly. The contrast between the two men was startling. One walked in the barren plains of self-interest; the other walked on higher ground.

What do you think Jesus, who rebuked James and John for their petty self-promotion, would say about our blatant scramble for denominational chief seats today? It sounds so much like the egotistic self-interest of the Sons of Thunder, doesn't it? "We've been left out, it's our turn to be elected, put us on the boards and committees, give us the positions." When shrewd brokers of power manipulate the democratic processes of this Convention in order to promote themselves, they've slipped from God's high ground to the barren plains of selfish ambition and conceit. And the Bible says, "Let nothing be done through selfish ambition or conceit, but in lowliness of mind let each esteem another better than himself."

We don't need "king of the mountain" competition today; we need compassionate cooperation. God didn't put us here to see through each other. He put us here to see each other through.

Did you hear about the two hikers who encountered a wild bear on the trail? One of them quickly sat down, took off his heavy hiking boots, reached in his backpack, and slipped on his running shoes. His companion said, "What are you doing? You know you can't outrun that bear." The other replied, "I don't have to outrun the bear. I just have to outrun you!"

We're not supposed to be outrunning each other, but standing together with each other against principalities and powers and the ruler of darkness and the hosts of wickedness in high places.

First Peter 5:5-6 says, "All of you be submissive to one another, and be clothed with humility, for God resists the proud, but gives grace to the humble. Therefore humble yourselves under the mighty hand of God, that He may exalt you in due time."

The first chapter of John's Gospel describes the first man to carry the name Baptist. He was the forerunner of Jesus. Jesus called him the greatest man who ever lived. But look again at that first chapter. Every reference to John the Baptist is one of personal depreciation. Verse 8 says, "He was *not* that light, but was sent to bear witness of that light." In verse 15 John the Baptist says of himself, "He who comes after me was before me. He has a higher rank than I have." He claims in verse 27, "He who comes after me is preferred before me. His sandal straps I am not worthy to unlatch."

John's enemies thought it would make him jealous when they told him in chapter 10 that Jesus was baptizing more people than he was. (What would some of our preachers say if they were told that a neighboring pastor reported more baptisms than they did?) John's response was, "I must decrease; He must increase." In John 1:20 a delegation from Jerusalem asked him, "Who are you?" His reply: "I am *not* the Christ. I'm not the prophet; I'm not even Elijah. I am a voice"—literally a *phono*—that's all, a voice.

Ask a compass, "Are you north?" No answer; it just swings its faithful arrow toward the magnetic pole and points. Ask John, "Are you the light?" No answer; he just turns his face toward Jesus and says, "Behold the Lamb of God." John made humility a sacred art form. He never filed an IRS tax return, but if he had, his "personal depreciation schedule" would have been a classic!

But isn't it a shame today when a person becomes the focus of his own ministry—when self-promotion, autocratic leadership styles, and success goals become our highest priorities? Or worse, isn't it tragic when a church begins to worship its pastor instead of the Lord who called him, focusing on the herald instead of the King! No matter how great your pastor is, he's not the light, he's just a *phono*, just a voice pointing to the true light, announcing the King whose sandals none of us is worthy to unlatch.

Let's reclaim that vanishing quality of humility that was personified by Jesus and lived out so convincingly by John, the first Baptist! Let's turn from the barren plains of egotistic self-interest to the higher ground of Christlike humility.

Conclusion

These are the three pleas of my message:

1. Let's turn from the misty flats of forced uniformity to the higher ground of autonomous individualism.
2. Let's turn from the muddy swamps of political coercion to the higher ground of spiritual persuasion.
3. Let's turn from the barren plains of egotistic self-interest to the higher ground of Christlike humility.

When Nehemiah, the cupbearer to King Artaxerxes, was busy obeying God's command to rebuild the walls around Jerusalem, he was tempted to turn from his lofty work to take up lesser pursuits. His response to that temptation is the one I pray Southern Baptists will give. It's in Nehemiah 6:3: "I am doing a great work and I cannot come down. Why should the work stop while I leave it and come down to you?"

Stay on the heights, Southern Baptists. You're involved in a great work. Stay close to the Lord and to the task He has called you to perform. Be faithful to your historic heritage. Don't dabble in controversies. Don't exhaust your energies arm-wrestling for denominational control. This Convention is too valuable to let it become a volleyball bounced back and forth across a political net by clever game players. Stay on the higher ground of spiritual persuasion, autonomous individualism, and Christlike humility where you belong.

Shakespeare was right: "They that stand high have many blasts to shake them." But when we stand high with Christ, those blasts will not be jealous pot shots we lob at each other; they will be Satan's blasts hurled in desperation against a united family of faith. And we won't be afraid, because we'll be with the one who promised to make us more than conquerors. We'll be on higher ground.

So, Southern Baptists, our prayer should be:

Lord, lift us up and let us stand,
By faith, on Heaven's tableland,
A higher plane than we have found,
Lord, plant our feet on higher ground.

Bibliography

Bibliography

Books on Civility

Anderson, Elijah. *Code of the Street: Decency, Violence, and the Moral Life of the Inner City.* New York: Norton, 1999.

Banks, Robert, and R. Paul Stevens. *The Complete Book of Everyday Christianity.* Downers Grove: InterVarsity Press, 1997.

Bolton, Robert. *People Skills: How to Assert Yourself, Listen to Others, and Resolve Conflicts.* New York: Touchstone, 1986.

Caldwell, Mark. *A Short History of Rudeness: Manners, Morals, and Misbehavior in Modern America.* New York: Picador, 1999.

Carter, Stephen L. *Civility: Manners, Morals and the Etiquette of Democracy.* New York: Basic, 1998.

Cuddihy, J. M. *The Ordeal of Civility.* New York: Basic Books, 1974.

Ciaramicoli, Arthur P., and Katherine Ketcham. *The Power of Empathy: A Practical Guide to Creating Intimacy, Self-Understanding, and Lasting Love.* New York: Plume, 2001.

Davis, Phyllis. *E2: Using the Power of Ethics and Etiquette in American Business.* Entrepreneur Press, 2003.

Dreher, Henry. *The Immune Power Personality: 7 Traits You Can Develop to Stay Healthy.* New York: Plume. 1996.

Forni, P. M. *Choosing Civility: The 25 Rules of Considerate Conduct.* New York: St. Martin's Press, 2002.

Goleman, Daniel. *Emotional Intelligence.* New York: Bantam, 1997.

————. *Working with Emotional Intelligence.* New York: Bantam, 1998.

Hallowell, Edward M. *Connect.* New York: Pantheon, 1999.

Kasser, Tim. *The High Price of Materialism.* Cambridge: Bradford, 2002.

Martin, Judith. *Miss Manners Rescues Civilization from Sexual Harassment, Frivolous Lawsuits, and Other Lapses in Civility.* New York: Crown, 1996.

Mouw, Richard J. *Uncommon Decency: Christian Civility in an Uncivil World.* Downers Grove: InterVarsity Press, 1989.

Nichols, Michael P. *The Lost Art of Listening: How Learning to Listen Can Improve Relationships.* New York: The Guilford Press, 1995.

Ornish, Dean. *Love & Survival: The Scientific Basis for the Healing Power of Intimacy.* New York: HarperCollins, 1998.

Peck, M. Scott. *The Road Less Traveled: A New Psychology of Love, Traditional Values and Spiritual Growth.* New York: Touchstone, 1979.

Pennebaker, James W. *Opening Up: The Healing Power of Expressing Emotions.* New York: The Guilford Press, 1997.

Post, Peggy, and Peter Post. *The Etiquette Advantage in Business.* New York: Harper Resource, 1999.

Randall, Peter. *Adult Bullying: Perpetrators and Victims.* London: Routledge, 1997.

Rouner, Leroy S., ed. *Civility.* Notre Dame: U. of Notre Dame Press, 2000.

Shelley, Bruce. *A Call to Christian Character: Toward a Recovery of Biblical Piety.* Grand Rapids: Zondervan, 1970.

Smedes, L. *Mere Morality: What God Expects from Ordinary People.* Grand Rapids: Eerdmans, 1983.

Tannen, Deborah. *You Just Don't Understand: Women and Men in Conversation.* New York: Ballantine, 1991.

Taylor, Shelley E. *The Tending Instinct: How Nurturing Is Essential to Who We Are and How We Live.* New York: Times, 2002.

Truss, Lynn. *Talk to the Hand.* New York: Gotham Books, 2005.

Wallis, Jim. *Who Speaks for God?: An Alternative to the Religious Right—A New Politics of Compassion, Community, and Civility.* Delacorte, 1996.

Washington, George. *Rules of Civility & Decent Behavior in Company and Conversation.* Bedford: Applewood Books, 1988.

Williams, Virginia, and Redford Williams. *Lifeskills: Eight Simple Ways to Build Stronger Relationships, Communicate More Clearly, and Improve Your Health.* New York: Times, 1998.

Bibliography
Articles on Civility

Abshsire, David M. "The Grace and Power of Civility." *Center for the Study of the Presidency,* Washington D.C. <www.thePresidency.org>.

Anderson, Kerby. "Character and Civility." *Probe Ministries International,* <http://www.leaderu.com/org/probe/docs/civility>.

Bourke, Dale Hanson. "Civility's Moral Imperative." *Religion News Service,* <www.texnews.com/1998/religion/bourke0530.html>.

Buchanan, John M. "Good Manners." *The Christian Century* 118/7 (28 February 2001): 3.

Gallant, Janet. *Simple Courtesies: How to Be a Kind Person in a Rude World.* Pleasantville: Reader's Digest, 1996.

Herrick, James A. "What Do We Mean by 'Civil Discourse?' A Biblical Model of Managing Disagreement." Pew Society Lecture, Hope College (1999).

Jacoby, Nicole. "Etiquette Crisis at Work." *CNN Financial Network,* <http://money.cnn.com/1999/11/29/1ife/q manners>.

Ketteler, Ronald. "Speaking the Truth in Love...Christian Civility." *The Messenger* (2001): 14.

Marty, Martin. "Can You Be Too Civil?" *The Christian Century* 114/8 (5 March 1997): 255.

McCarthy, Abigail. "Mind Your Manners: It Makes Civilization Possible." *Commonweal* 76/10 (21 May 1999): 8.

No author. "Aggravating Circumstances: A Status Report on Rudeness in America." <www.publicagenda.org> (2005).

Stewart, Mark. "Restoring Civility." *The Washington Times,* (17 October 2000), 1.

Wallis, Jim. "A Crisis of Civility." *Sojourners Magazine* 25/5 (September-October, 1996): 16-21.